CRIME AND PUNISHMENT IN ENGLAND
1850–1922

Thirty titles published in facsimile documenting the dramatic changes in the extent and character of crime and society's attitudes toward criminals during the period

Edited by
Martin J. Wiener
RICE UNIVERSITY

A GARLAND SERIES

THE GAOL CRADLE
WHO ROCKS IT?

Benjamin Waugh

Garland Publishing, Inc.
New York & London
1984

For a complete list of the titles in this series see the final pages of this volume.

This facsimile has been made from a copy in the Library of Congress.

Library of Congress Cataloging in Publication Data

Waugh, Benjamin.
The Gaol Cradle, Who Rocks It?

(Crime and punishment in England, 1850–1922)
Reprint. Originally published: London : Strahan, 1873.
1. Juvenile delinquency—England. 2. Juvenile justice, Administration of—Great Britain. I. Title. II. Series.
HV9146.A5W38 1984 364.3′6′0942 83-49233
ISBN 0-8240-6208-6 (alk. paper)

The volumes in this series are printed on acid-free, 250-year-life paper.

Printed in the United States of America

THE GAOL CRADLE

WHO ROCKS IT?

THE GAOL CRADLE

Who Rocks It?

STRAHAN AND CO.
56 LUDGATE HILL LONDON
1873

PRINTED BY
TAYLOR AND CO., LITTLE QUEEN STREET,
LINCOLN'S INN FIELDS.

CONTENTS.

Part III.—Poverty.

INTRODUCTION.

It may appear presumptuous to publish opinions on such wide subjects as Juvenile Crime, Inoccupation, and Poverty, based upon limited observation.

Too many in every department of knowledge, are apt to imitate the cockney—who, late on a dark night, alighting from a coach at Brighton, engaged the stable boy to accompany him to the jetty with the stable lantern and rope, that by the cord-suspended lantern he might "see the sea," and, returning home early in the morning, announced to his companion on the box that he had "seen the sea!—the mighty deep which bears the commerce of the world!" It must be admitted that not a few of the illustrious cockney's followers are to be found in departments of knowledge which specially affect the interests of the poor.

Philosophers, politicians, philanthropists, and novelists, with the fluent tongue speak, and with the ready pen write, of these great questions, utterly innocent of the fact that after all they are but the cockney on the literary coach box; by their stable lantern have they seen the sea.

If the limitedness of my observation should lay me open to a like charge, I shall be at least introduced into a not undistinguished circle. But after all, it is possible so closely to observe a small cupful of water from the sea, so carefully to analyse it, and so fairly to weigh the results as to render the work not altogether without scientific value; to borrow the language of logicians, to gain in intention what you lose in extension. In some measure, at least, my observation fulfils this condition, and its conclusions are on me as a great woe.

One cannot take up a newspaper without reading that certain juveniles have gone to gaol. With what object do you send them? The question, I venture to think, lies at the bottom of a great social reform. Beginning with things as they are, what is gaol? What is your idea of a thoroughly efficient gaol? What is the end to the inmates and to the community?

The chief object of this book is to enforce the idea that the actual mission of gaol is to select the strongest natures of the neglected young, and work on them a bad transformation;—that its actual mission is, in short, to rock its own cradle.

As a kindred subject—the main reel from which the dark thread of crime is spun—the inoccupation of the young of the poor forms a part of this book; and the subjects of poverty, and laws for poverty, because affecting the morale and chances of the children of poverty, have a minor place.

It may be just to say that, though I have written with emphasis, I have not had opportunities of knowledge save such as are open to all who care to use them.

I should like to have reserved this book until more extensive observation had given it greater completeness,—until its opinions could have been supported by a larger number of facts; but, remembering that the opinions it advances find an *a priori* argument in axioms interwoven with our most familiar household words, that the national mind is especially alive to the interests of the young of the masses, that the greatest work now in the people's hand is the work of adapting our national institutions to their wants, I have ventured to publish it as it is, in the hope that it may not be without service at least in the direction of enquiry.

London, 1873.

PART I.—CRIME.

CHAPTER I.

JUVENILE ENORMITIES IN STREET AND PARLOUR.

WITH respect to the ordinary, day-by-day, little street-rough, I have observed two distressful results of legislative action. It first names him black, then makes him black; or, to change the figure and carry it a little further, it calls him a dog, it makes him a dog, and then it hangs him.

Perchance the reader has seen, and been able to analyse a whole year's list of juvenile crime. When you saw it, did it strike you that between the raw propensities of the happy and of the hapless British juvenile there was a wonderful similarity? Excuse the enquiry; the fact is so often forgotten. Did you then consider the harsh and tyrannical conditions under which street-life is lived, and make fair allowance for these? The performance of even this small act of common fairness is frequently forgotten. Having done this, I am sure you found with astonishment, that the half of the so-called "crime" list is something like humbug.

If it were not so serious a matter, it might not be worth while to show that the legal names given to the actions of our "urchin" citizens, all approved authorities on jurisprudence notwithstanding, are duping, juggling affairs. But legal names excite false opinions, evoke feelings of horror out of all proportion to the facts of the case, mistify and muddle some of the gravest questions of the day, distort the judgment, and restrain and repress the best tendencies of the true English heart.

It may be worth while, therefore, to hold the law at a respectful distance whilst we look at the following analysis of "juvenile crime." The analysis is of *first* "crimes," and first "crimes" only. The data are supplied by the highest authority, and apply to children dragged up from a group of miserable dens, in which the analyst took a philosophical interest, and where juvenile crime was the cardinal crime. Out of every hundred "villains" led up to the magistrate's court, sixty-five were juveniles: one specimen actually appeared at the mature age of six.

It seems too absurd to be true that stealing a tart is legal felony!—that the young appetitive urchin is legally a felon!

Dropping, therefore, the thralling technicalities of the law, let us enquire of what enormities a representative band of these urchins have been guilty?

Twenty-three have sinned sins of feeling; with their passions aroused, they have damaged somebody or something. Imagine, doating father, what would be the consequence if your strongly-excitable boy should change places with the strong-impulsed boy of the streets. Consider, should your own brave and fiery Master Charley, under excitement, hurl a heavy toy at the head of peevish, provoking Master Harry, and striking, break the skin of his cheek, or missing, break the glass of the window. Then imagine Policeman A. 27, as his appointed nurse, dropping the fatal hand upon his little shoulder. Charley, changed not in nature but in lot, would become a unit to the year's list of "Juvenile Criminals," and serve to dismalise the visage of some excellent and sincere Exeter Hall orator, and to impart a sensational shock to an Exeter Hall audience. Charley, the impulsive lad, of whose very failings you are secretly proud, would, instead of simply being whipped and sent to bed, be conveyed to a prison or to a reformatory, to be fed and lodged at public charge, in five years to swell the reports of "turned out well."

Not to be expressed are the feelings with which, in the name of all common sense, you would resent such a thing. But can that which would be injustice,—absurd, atrocious injustice,—to your Charley cease to be absurd, atrocious injustice, when applied to the Charley of your charwoman!

Thirty-three of these juvenile humanities were guilty of sins of appetite. They were charged with taking bread, fruit, sweets, or other luxuries or necessities of life, without their respective owner's permission.

It may not be rude to our respectable readers to ask whether they can conscientiously say that they never, at any time in their childhood when appetite coincided with opportunity, erred upon this point. And what if the plums that conquered your virtue had been the property of an angry stranger, who believed in justice, and at whose service the State had placed the strong arm of her law—policeman, stipendiary, and gaol!

We should, in twenty-four hours, have sent you to gaol. On your entry, we should have taken due note of name, age, height, complexion, occupation. Then we should have shorn your head, bathed you, changed your clothes, given you a cell, appointed you your work; and in the morning, clad in the prison dress —one half the weight of your own—in the open air, perhaps in the depth of winter, set you, hammer in hand, to break stones. In the afternoon we should have set you to pick oakum, and have taken from you breakfast and supper if you failed to pick the allotted weight. In the middle of your first exercise of stone breaking, you would probably have dropped your hammer and begun to cry; forthwith, your ears would have been boxed. "What's that for?" you would have said, not having yet learnt to accept unquestioningly the tyrannical discipline of the prison. Whereupon, we should have led you to the Governor, who would have resented the troublesome intrusion, and punished the offence. Through a long weary month, we should have made you break and pick your tale of stones and oakum; fed you on so many ounces of bread, and so many pints of water or gruel per diem; punished you if you laughed, punished you if you cried, punished you if you spoke, punished you if you looked behind you; and addressed you in the same brow-beating tone used to the stoutest villain in penal servitude—and then we should have turned you out; and then what! Try to imagine it!

To what extent is His Worship on the bench there indebted for his present grade in society, to the fact that *his* young virtue failed him at the door of mamma's side-board, not at a baker's window; and to what extent does that hulking, thievish-looking fellow just sent to Newgate owe his grade in society, to the fact that *his* young virtue failed at the counter of a confectioner's shop, he being fatherless! In what differing moods must these two think of their "Auld Lang Syne?"

Nine of these our batch of youngsters were guilty of mere freaks, such as letting off fire-works where they should not, striding a horse and, through too keen a sense of "the glory of motion," riding furiously.

Seven were little beggars or tramps.

Thirty-one had sinned through avarice. They were charged with stealing money, or goods which might be turned into money. Imagine one who seldom touched a copper, hearing a comrade's glorious story of the Pantomime, or smelling on a cold night the delicious fragrance of a hot potato, coming suddenly and unexpectedly on a chance of for once gratifying his desire, and how need he be an utter villain to fall into temptation. Neighbouring fairs, theatres, travelling shows, and even innocent provision dealers were not without a share in sapping this juvenile integrity. To own a knife, to see a play, or even to grasp a tart, is the *summum bonum* of many a penniless lad. For such objects, in moments of tormenting desire, he runs the risk of the gaol.

Not being mere maudlin moralists, men who look sometimes see in the circumstances of a "theft" things that betoken subjects for philanthropic hopeful work. But not so the law.

The cases of six of the biggest of these little "thieves" I am able to particularise.

On the day which chronicled the capture and incarceration of the first of these dangerous mortals, there might have been seen, lounging in a low street, a pale, shrivelled, languid-looking boy of twelve and a half. His father a waterman, his mother a waterman's wife, a passable couple as the street went. How he was employed no one knew. How he was not employed everybody knew. He was neither at school, at home, nor at work. He gave no trouble to his parents and made no noise in the street. Up to the time when he was taken by the police he had the good fortune, singular in his class, to bear no reputation. Why did he steal? Strolling about, he saw a garden-door open and a tame rabbit within. He "coursed" it, caught it, and sold it. He is one of many who, in some unlucky moment, steal as the stars are said to shine—"Because they 've nothing else to do." Reader, was he thus proved to be hopelessly bad?

Entering a small yard by a long passage leading out of a narrow low street, we pass upstairs to the top room of a dingy, tumble-down house, let out in flats. The room contains a fire-grate, a window-frame a little glazed, the rest stuffed with rags or nailed up with the staves of a demolished tub, a heap of filthy rags called a bed, and a gaudy picture of the Saviour. This murky place has a free circulation of air. Once it had a ceiling, but the lath and plaster ruin had ceased to be worthy of that name. The stars look through the tiles, and there is no door. Here the second of our young thieves lived with a younger brother. His mother, a widow it was supposed, got her living nobody knew how. She paid monthly visits to the boys, and then settled for the room and for the two pounds of potatoes served to them hot on a tray every morning: every other requisite they found for themselves. Why did he steal? The night before the theft—a clear, still, bitter night—the thief-to-be lay with his brother coiled up in their rag bed. Rising to a fireless grate and a fuelless cupboard, the shivering creature set out to get something to warm their den. Ice prevented his picking coal at low water from the Thames bank, so he stole a small bag full from a coal-yard. Reader, was he an abandoned wretch?

Ill, in lodgings, with a kindly old woman, so reputed among homeless boys, to whom he paid ninepence per week, might be seen the boy who became the third thief. For some reason—the cruelty of his step-father, he said—he had left his home, and had started in the world on his "own hook" at the early age of twelve. His income arose from sweeping at a crossing, and now and then carrying parcels for passengers from the railway station. Why did he steal? Whilst laid aside, his rent got a fortnight into arrears. Bad times made it difficult for him to meet his current wants, and impossible to pay off the old score. The woman was kind, but the little fellow did not like to be in her debt. He stole empty wine bottles from the yard of a gentleman's house, sold them for one shilling and ninepence, took the money to the woman, and said, "Here is your money, Sally; and threepence to be going on with." Reader, was he an utter villain?

Singing at the doors of gin-palaces, might sometimes be heard the voice of a tawny foreign-looking boy. His father, a box-organ grinder, has been some weeks dead. He is a general favourite in the neighbourhood, especially at the lodging-house, where, on the morning of the very day on which he attained one of those social distinctions which entitle to the notice of the British Press, it is said that he shared his morning meal with some aged tramp. And why did he steal? He was in love, and imagined his loved one would look better in a brooch; at all events, he had the fatal feeling that it would gratify her to have a present from him. He took the girl to a small brooch-dealer's shop window, she selected, and he romantically vowed that the next time they met the brooch should be hers. To buy it was impossible. The shop was one where the master both sold and worked. Leading out of this was a door, half-glazed and the glass was half-covered with a muslin curtain. Behind the door was a living-room. The critical opportunity at length came. The street-door was ajar, the master was at dinner, the brooch within three steps and an arm's length! Softly he enters, gently he stretches out his hand, the brooch is his, when, unluckily for the tawny boy, something falls, the master is after him, and in a few minutes—

"Love's labour lost,"

the lad is in the hands of the police. Reader, was he unredeemably bad?

The fifth is a tall boy of thirteen, little more than skin and skeleton. Why did he steal? From sheer hunger. For a butcher was his victim, and his prize he ate raw. Reader, was he a vicious ruin?

The last is a good-looking, eager boy. Why did he steal? A tenth-rate greengrocer in a low part of the town had roused the ire of the neighbourhood by cruelty to a servant-girl. After cursing the man somewhat freely, the boys resolved on doing him damage. At the side of his window hung a board announcing the price of coals, and "Orders received within." That board must be taken. One lad addressing another, said, "Cabb, you loved her, you're the man." Cabb was not forward to respond; but, "O, Cabb's a coward; he's a jelly heart;" and "Cabb's no coward; he's game, boys—he's game," put the requisite mettle into him. He was dared to do, and he risked to suffer. Reader, was he utterly depraved?

In all these cases save the fifth, I saw the State start what I am convinced is a legalised havoc of character and life chances, havoc ever increasing until the victim—unless the grave stop the tragedy,—stands before its tribunal to receive its final award, a gaunt figure with dark haggard face and fiendish eye. Prison was the process, the people's taxes were the cost. But of this in another place.

To return to the list. What with the character of the streets and dwellings whence they came; what with the habits of their parentage and association; what with the idleness forced upon all children who are ill-fed and ill-clothed; what with the instinctive appetites and passions they have in common with all boyish flesh and blood; what with the unnatural and indescribable privations of their untended lives, perilous to every faculty of body, mind, and heart, their cases can only excite commiseration; and that we were skilful enough to capture, and strong enough to punish this one hundred and three young creatures, is a matter of very gloomy satisfaction. The wonderfulness of this company lies, not in its criminal performances, but in its possessing any semblance of morality. Nevertheless for a lad who cannot work a moral miracle, an eager and vulgar justice, blind to all remoter consequences, prescribes punishments which are simply a horrid wrong.

This beginning of imprisonment is in every aspect a solemn affair.

Can the reader say whether there are such things in human beings as innate ideas? Do they not rush out on certain actions, and call them unjust unequivocally? Is this law suspended in the man to whom as a child you give an absurdly unjust name, and mete out an awfully unjust punishment? Does it not seem possible, at least, that a criminal class, being translated, will be a revengeful class—and wrong the community because by the community having been irremediably wronged? Is it not by a law, cogent as any other law, that in a reckless manhood the child takes his unconscious, inevitable revenge? Think you the homely words of a too-little-heeded teacher, "With what measure ye mete, it shall be measured to you again," may not, after all, apply to State wrongs done to a child?

Some bright and shining lights of science somewhere have said that their religion—or whatever it should be called—is "to find out natural law and then live by it." What better could possess them than to turn the jet of their thought, their most fervent, most brilliant thought, on the "harem-scarem" of the street. So doing, may they not light up a dark and dismal question, and find out whether the form of villany specially assumed by the biggest villains who inhabit our gaols and hulks, is anything more than human nature developed, branded, devilised by police law.

Science would indeed be a gospel if she concentrated her power on the street child on the way to gaol. Let but the principles which she now so eagerly applies to the nature and development of *Globigerinæ*, be as eagerly and honestly applied to the fragments of humanity which are found in the London slums, and possibly some of the many forms of evil into which they develop—evils confounding statesmen and making patriots weep—would fade away into the historical obscurity which shrouds those minute geological remains of a long-gone-bye world.

Perchance my reader is a mere ordinary citizen, a fastidious supporter of moral law—(if such readers can have read so far)—sitting judge over the police news of his morning paper. Two things I would say to him. First, it is not true that to the ragged character of the streets, distance lends enchantment. In these cases ignorance is the secret of harsh judgment, as it is of blundering legislation also. On acquaintance even the gravest cases appear to be partially excusable.

The rigid application of a code of lofty morals well befits you sitting in self-judgment. It *may* befit you, too, sitting in judgment on the delinquent member of your own well-trained, well-fed, well-loved family; but the same process applied to any one child in this unfortunate hundred and three befits only the iciest Pharisee. For simple injustice and lack of all that is truly manly, the proceeding has few rivals. Yet how is it that nine out of ten Englishmen to-day believe that their own personal integrity is in some way proved by their acting in this stupid manner towards the pitiable outcast, and that the proceeding is in itself a kind of homage to Good ?

CHAPTER II.

STARTED FOR THE HULKS—JUST INJUSTICE.

WHATEVER can possess the country to be contented with its present Criminal Law? Surely there must be in the popular mind lack of all knowledge and lack of all interest, or this contentment could not last one day longer. We know that there is a police court; we read about it; read that its officers take up and send to prison beggars, and fighters, and thieves, and we are glad of it; but, were we better informed, how often should we blush at its services as only legalized atrocities!

Fairly consider the following events, taken from the lawful proceedings of English officials who dominate the poor-boy world by virtue of authority that you and I have given, and judge them without shame, if you can.

I see no reason why they should not be regarded as a fair tableaux of events counted by thousands.

* * * * * *

Passing out of a small pawnbroker's shop is a woman of middle height, pale, somewhat haggard, and evidently in keen mental distress. The shop is of necessity lit with gas though mid-day. It is entered by three steps, down which the woman's transit into the street is made with more than usual speed by some energetic and unfriendly impulse from within, accompanied by a volley of expletives more emphatic than euphonious. The altercation which ensues explains the occasion :—

"You know it isn't, you villain! you swindling villain!" said the almost breathless woman the moment she had landed on the causeway. There was no mere irritation in the words. The tone was full, the lip quivered, the eye moistened; the deepest and best in the woman trembled in her words: "You swindling villain!"

"Go away you ——! you ——! or I'll give you in charge," said the pawnbroker, coming from within the cavernous depths of clothing and carpets which lined the way up into the gas-lit shop. Fixing his fierce eyes full on the woman, he continued, "You've got your own, you lying ——! What would you have, perhaps your pick; that's what you want, is it?"

For a moment she turned a fixed, inquiring gaze on the third finger of her left hand with her very soul in her eyes, then she looked up at the broker, and in a flood of hysterical tears, shrieked, "It isn't it, it isn't! It isn't it!"

A week or so before, this unfortunate woman had at this shop pawned her wedding-ring. Sixteen sad years it had been hers. Less than a year after marriage, by the capsizing of a boat, the man who gave it her was buried in the sea. After the birth of her child she almost lost the use of one leg, which circumstance might account for her subsequent long widowhood. Forced by stress of winter's want, she had for the first time yielded to what had been through the years an oft-repeated temptation, and temporarily raised money by this dismal and, as it turned out, disastrous expedient. The struggle, she said, was severe, and her manner of saying it compelled belief.

At the very first possible moment the honest little woman hurried off to redeem. Vividly to convey to paper the flood of deadly thoughts and feelings which surged in upon her in that moment when the long-familiar eye detected a difference between the ring restored and the ring pledged, when to the testimony of the eye the long-familiar finger lent the testimony of feeling, is impossible. The woman's soul was suddenly one dense and awful woe, a fact which the candid and wifely reader may not altogether fail to apprehend.

Whether the woman's impression was true to fact or false to fact, whether the ring was the same ring "sweated," or another ring, and of lighter weight, we have no opinion; but that it was not the veritable ring there can be no doubt.

At half-past six on the same day the only child of the distressed woman came home for his tea. He was a mop-headed, manful lad, fifteen years old; had for his age ample flesh and blood, was kind to his mother, and could work with a will and eat with the same. In a boiler-maker's yard, where he had recently obtained employment to pick up bolts and do odd jobs in general, his hands won the chief portion of the family's precarious income. His few shillings wage he always paid in full to his mother. Through his strong, untaught, and often unemployed life not a tongue in the court had seriously pronounced against his conduct. He was a straight-forward, ignorant, well-meaning fellow.

When he entered the room his mother was nursing her sorrow with a quiet cry. "What's up, mother; what's up now?" said the lad roughly suiting his noisy voice and boisterous manner to the sacredness of the occasion.

The story was soon given, and, pointing to the ring, now taken from the finger and put on the mantelpiece, she concluded, "I shall never wear it again." By the tale and the tears all that was in the lad—filial love, justice, poetry (a wonderful element, by the way, in the ruder, braver spirits of the streets)—was roused to indignation. His face paled, he bit his lips, he muttered hard names and awful threats; he hurriedly swallowed his tea, put the ring in his pocket, seized his cap, and without staying to consider means or consequences, without one trace of mean-spirited calculating wisdom, he went out, slamming the door behind him, and entered the street, saying, as he did so, "I'll set it right." Following the strongest of his instincts and the best of his knowledge, with a just cause, a brave heart, and a good fist, the lad proceeded direct to the pawnbroker's shop.

Here he found his victim, a thin, steely-visaged man of forty or forty-five, of middle height, pacing about beneath the hanging lighted lamps on the pavement opposite his shop window.

Not a moment was wasted. With the force of that earnestness which, in six minutes from the first hearing of his mother's wrong, had enabled him to swallow a meal and leave behind him nearly half a mile, the avenger at once demanded his mother's ring.

"How do I know who's your mother?" fenced the pawnbroker.

"Where's my mother's ring," persisted the boy.

The pawnbroker seemed to be searching his memory.

"You don't know, don't you!" continued the lad clearing his throat, phlegmy with the heat of suppressed rage. "Give me my mother's ring, you swindling thief."

In language which, at least, in the range and vigour of its epithets, altogether surpassed the not very choice language of his excited accuser, the man declared that his mother had got her ring, and declared something else besides, which something else seriously compromised her character.

The pawnbroker had gone too far; all that was lacking in vehemence of indignation was now supplied by the double wronger of his mother's ring and his mother's name,—fists and feet fell fast; then, by fair play or by foul play, blood fell too; then the combatants fell, and muttered curses mingled with the blows.

Meanwhile a crowd had gathered; children stood agape, big lads, pleased with the pluck, cried "Go it, young un." But the cause of the strife nobody knew.

"What's all this about?" said a big square-built man in buttoned-up-blue, suddenly pressing through the crowd.

The combatants had just risen. Coming on

him from behind, the lad saw not the official form, and, intent on his one end, heard not the official tone. The policeman grasping the lad by his collar, he struck out behind to gain his freedom and pressed forward with the cry, "Give me that ring." By a shake of the gigantic arm he suddenly awoke to his dreadful fate.

"I did not know it was you," timidly weazed the almost strangled lad.

"I give him into charge for battery and assault," said the pawnbroker. "I was a doing nothing, and he at me like a tiger," he continued in a piteous and injured tone.

"He did," cried an excited woman, perhaps the pawnbroker's wife.

"A young fiend," murmured another.

"He wants the treadmill," cried a third.

At this point an intelligent and well-dressed citizen, who had come up with the crowd, and who, by converse with some of its outsiders, had got an inkling of the whole affair, ventured to ask the lad himself, now pale and subdued, "Why did you meddle with the man? What about this ring?"

"I'll tell you why," frankly began the palpitating boy, when the autocrat of the street, who now had him "in custody," magisterially put a stop to the reply by, "That's no business of mine," and led away the boy to the station to enter the "charge" for "to-morrow's hearing."

And thus the heroic avenger of a mother's wrong blundered into gaol. There, in execution of his original sentence, you gave him day-by-day for three months the hard labour of a prison; to which you added, for breaches of conventional prison law, an unusual number of cuffs on the ear, and special starvation diet, and dark-cell punishments. A well-disposed lad, he felt more keenly the ignominy of his lot; especially was he provoked to indignant rebellion by the dictatorial manner of his keeper. Quiet, hardworking, and honest, he was hot-blooded, and could not stand injustice. Your sending him here was an injustice, and he felt it; but to be struck for merely looking behind him added insult to injury, and he resented it. In a moment his hot blood was insolent. Then you gave him the dark cell, reduced his diet, and gave him an extra round at the mill. At the end of his service you were glad to get rid of him, but predicted as the gate shut him out into the street, "That gentleman will be here again!"

And how can you wonder that such a lad, repressed, rendered helpless, and maddened by the power of such long-continued discipline, seeing through it neither your good intention nor correct administration, should say in his deepest heart this was a grievous wrong—should play a bad part in life and find his way to gaol again!

Does the gaoler's forecast seem altogether unnatural; and, if you who maddened and branded him were the only sufferer, would it be altogether undeserved? In such circumstances, given a soul, and surely in the nature of things some sort of ruin must be inevitable.

The verifier o the particulars knows nothing more of the boy than this—that on his exit from gaol, after fruitless endeavours to regain his situation, which had been filled, and fruitless endeavours to obtain another, he and his mother left their old neighbourhood, probably hoping to "start again."

God help the heedless chivalry of the streets! Every day the State is busy, by vast machinery and lavish expenditure, capturing and cursing it. Well is it for the writer and for not a few of his respectable readers that their boyish days were passed under the discriminating reign of a schoolmaster. I should like to know where had been the noble, the daring, the rash, the generous soul had they fought their indignation fights against cowards and sneaks under the resistless and undiscriminating dominion which sways its sceptre over the enthusiastic child of the street.

Judge your law in another case!

"The mother's dead; the boy has gone to gaol!" Thus spoke a Relieving Officer to a Board of Guardians in explanation of 4*s*. 8*d*. which was not now needed for out-door relief.

"Mother dead." She had been dying eleven months, and should have been bed-ridden all that time, but had dragged about till within the last few weeks. For twelve years after her faithless husband abandoned her, she took in washing. Those years had been a long weary struggle against ill-health. Finally, cancer conquered the honest creature, and laid her on a pauper's bed. At two o'clock in the morning, alone, on the sacking-bottom of a four-post bed, she died!

Three days before she died, her only child—a boy—went out to beg. Cancer has a mighty hunger. To its wants, parish allowance was nothing. The boy did not take kindly to begging, was naturally proud; but he loved his mother, and love conquered. The narrow, filthy street had in it scarcely a noisier or kindlier soul. He set out on his expedition. In two days—eleven miles away from home, unwashed and hungry-looking, he stood before a magistrate, charged with begging and having five shillings in his pocket! He was committed for three months with hard labour, the magistrate observing, "We *must* put a stop to this sort of thing."

* * * * * *

It is getting dark. The latch of the door of a second-floor room—where sit a man, his wife, and two children round a table with a candle and tea-things on it—is quietly lifted.

"Who's there?" said a kindly voice.

"I was looking for my mother," timidly replied the intruder.

"Your mother! I know what you want, you gaol-bird! Out! you skulking thief!"

The kindly tone had changed to thunder. The shorn head, the pale face stamped the inquirer a villain, and the voice, sounding dishonest through shaking cold and hunger, gave emphasis to the appearance. He shut the door, and quickly gained the street. At a small coal-shop he learnt that his mother was dead. The lad cried so bitterly that the woman-keeper of it gave him a crust of bread and some tea; but she was an upright woman, had heard of his going to gaol for stealing, and told him to clear off.

* * * * * *

On a clear November midnight, a policeman on the bank of the Thames found a poor, ill-clad fellow, of some sixteen years of age, nearly dead with cold! The policeman took him to the station. A few days later, he might be seen using an axe in a philanthropic chip-yard where he fed and slept. Here Christian visitors took deep interest in the objects of their charity. And not a week passed without a visitor, and none visited the yard after the new boy's arrival without the shorn head attracting attention, exciting inquiry, receiving solution, evoking advice.

"And who is this?" said a circular gentleman, of most agreeable manner and moderate attachment to the snuff-box, as he addressed the master. The story was given—begging and gaol!

"Well, my boy," said the kindly gentleman in a solemn tone, "it's a sad thing to break your country's law; all sin is against God; you must never do it again."

"But did we not hear that he did it for his mother?"

"Yes, sir, I did," said the lad.

"Well, then, my boy, you were a brave fellow; I would have done the same. Do your best, and I'll befriend you!"

Three months of gaol meditation on wrong done to him, that wrong now the reason for kicks from his own class and well-meant sermons, but not a word of sympathy from Christians; these things had crushed the young lad. He was morose, gloomy, half-reckless. Is it not sometimes forgotten by those who wear the name of Christ, that He came not to condemn, because He came to redeem. Lecturing degrades, sympathy elevates. In every grade and in every sphere—

> "Men may o'erget delusion—not despair."

The moment that the lad felt another life in unison with his own, was the birth of hope—that frail yet majestic thing, that chief of conquerors.

"Tell me how he gets on," said this new friend, addressing the master, "and whether he is worthy of a better place, and he shall have it."

The lad was equal to the opportunity. Twelve months hence he was apprenticed to a skilled handicraft. Industry, night-school, Sabbath evening service, natural tact, and master's kindness made up his first few months in his new world. In very early days his wages were advanced; then he filled a post of some little responsibility, in which hard and brave endeavour found a worthy reward. Reasonable visions of the future were bright. Then it became known by the workmen that he had been in gaol, and with this knowledge came the lad's greatest difficulty—the lofty morality of the British workman! His lot became unbearable. To render a reproof pungent, to account for aught missing there was henceforth no difficulty. Suddenly he decamped. To his friend he said, in keenest despair, "I could do anything if men were like you."

He enlisted for a soldier. At the 'Three Bells,' the head-quarters of the enlisting officer, he was seen by a workman who sat soaking his brains in beer.

"That lad," said he to the sergeant, when the lad had gone out, "that lad's apprentice to a customer of mine. I suppose he's cut his sticks. They say as he's been in gaol."

At night, the sergeant, who had often been drunk, but had never been in gaol, asked, "What gaol were you in, old fellow?"

From business he had fled to be rid of that wretched spectre. It is at him again.

The maddened recruit absconded. He was captured, tried, and gaoled again. In a letter to his friend he said, "This is a damned world."

* * * * * *

Perhaps the reader is weak as the writer, and feels half disposed to echo the sentiment. It was a hard judgment, but, from his standpoint, a right one notwithstanding.

But do not forget the cause in the case. Every day in the police-courts of cities, towns, villages, from Land's End to John o' Groats, like deadly work is being done. Countless agents have it as their duty to proceed against ignorant and foolish youth, by all the powers of law to destroy visions, madden passions, and cripple a whole life's power, — to inflict, in short, tremendous unimaginable wrong!

I am not able further to follow the thread of this melancholy life. On the general question of an imprisoned boy's destiny, the following circumstance is not without significance.

The scene is the common cell of a Police Court. Eight criminals are awaiting their trial. The moment is that in which, after alighting from the black van, which collected them from various stations, they have just made each other's acquaintance. Their ages range from forty-three to sixteen.

"Well youngster, an' what may you be here for?" jauntily said a strong, well-built young fellow of about twenty-two. "Never here afore, my hearty? O, well, you'll be here oft enough, I'll tell you!"

"You should know better than talk in that way to a boy in trouble" said the oldest of the company."

"What's up?" cheerfully interrupted the young fellow, "what's the use of a lecturing? We're all in trouble, I shan't harm the lad, not I!"

"You shouldn't talk to a boy like that; he'd better work for an honest living, and not come here again."

"On my soul! you're a good fellow. I like you rarely. What are you here for, may I be so bold as to ask?"

"I'm here because I can't pay a debt!"

"Lord bless me! It seems as everybody comes here sooner or later. Its but the other day as I was up for my first hearing, such another as that lad; what's yo'r age, youngster?"

"Sixteen! Ah! yo'r little o' your age. I was thirteen when they took me for taking a shilling from a till. I've been six times up since then, an' I've done one 'stretch' in —— prison; an' now I reckon, I'll get fourteen years; an' I don't care if its twenty. They'll send me to ——, to take my trial at th' 'ssizes."

"Why doesn't a strong young fellow like you work like an honest man?" said the debtor.

"Work! The Lord knows all about work! Work! when you've been to prison; who'll have you? Work! I said work when I served for that shilling; but work!" Here he stood up, began to whistle, and walked to the other end of the cell, as though by a whistle he would keep from something else — in which effort he was not quite successful, and so turned his face away, professing to be looking out of the grated, waved-glass window.

The cell-door opened for one of the prisoners to go into court. The young fellow turned from the window, and said sharply to the officer, who then made his appearance,

"Has anybody come?"

The officer knew what he meant, and replied, "Yes."

"Is it — ?" said he in excited and subdued tone.

The door was shut, and the officer gone, before any reply.

The questioner named the name of a warder who would probably come down from the prison in which he had served his last conviction.

"Good heavens! What if it's him! I did rather it was anybody than ——. He's the best man alive; I promised him I'd mend. Well, I tried; God knows, I tried; but its no use—no work and mending won't go."

This, and more of a like character, he half sighed, half said, and then turning to the lad, continued,

"Ah! youngster. I wish they'd hear me for you; once in an' its no use. I'd go on me knees for you; what have you been after?"

The key of the cell turned again. The door opened and the warder most dreaded appeared.

"Bob! Bob!" said the good fellow in a strong, soft, almost womanly tone.

Every nerve in Bob's face twitched. There was a great melting and heaving. After swallowing something, Bob went forward, and putting his hand familiarly on the warder's shoulder, said, as best he could, " It isn't your —your fault—I wish I was done for."

The man who at first reproved Bob for his apparently reckless style of address, a month afterwards, in closing his narrative to the writer with evident disturbance of lip said, " I didn't believe that I could have loved a man in that time."

Let this fragment tell its own tale.

Once he took his master's shilling, possibly was wretched the moment he had done it, willing to do anything to undo it, yet in the shilling's owner he found no place for repentance. Because he sinned against a harsh man, you imprisoned him, and sent him back to the world out of which he had come, branded, doomed. And whom did you serve?

The boy?

The master?

The community?

In passing it may be worth while to ask what must be the educational influence of such events on the people whose foolish sons you thus wrong? Can it prepare them to love justice, revere laws, and honour the Crown? Towards these things, will it not be well if it breed only apathy, but how can it fail to breed hate?

CHAPTER III.

QUESTIONS WITHOUT ANSWERS.

It surely can be no breach of good faith to insert here the following questions and answers. The circumstances in which they originated are recited only to show how little is known of the stages through which the greatest criminals pass to their melancholy end.

One Sunday afternoon a rough scholar in a Sunday school is turned out into the street for striking somebody. There and then he seizes on the nearest thing to his hand and smashes the school window. He is given into the custody of the police and sent to prison.

Some years after this, in the quiet of the early morning, a young man is led from the condemned cell of a gaol. He stands upon the drop, the noose is fixed,—a moment of dreadful silence—the youth is dying, a few moments more and the struggling lad is dead.

Next morning the execution was announced in every paper throughout the land. In due course the Home Secretary laid upon the table of the House of Commons the bill for the costs of this piece of public service, and asked the representatives of the people to provide the money. They met the demand, provided the money and the whole thing was done with.

Hearing that the hanged youth had been an inhabitant of his own district; that there he had begun his prison history; that this history began, too, as a boy, and in the event recited above, the writer asked the police authorities of the district kindly to furnish him with the following particulars:—the *age* at which the lad was first convicted, the nature of the *charge* and the sentence given, also the same particulars of the subsequent convictions. At the same time a request was made for like information as to FIVE lads whom the district had reared for penal servitude.

The local authorities replied politely, informed the querist that the information desired was not at their disposal, and directed him to apply to the office of Habitual Criminals.

The application was accordingly made with the following result:—

4, Whitehall Place.

Sir,—I have to acknowledge the receipt of your letters of the —— and —— inst., requesting to be furnished with particulars of the convictions of ——, who was hanged some time ago, and the convictions of —— who have gone from ——, also with certain details respecting Habitual Criminals; and, in reply, I have to refer you to the Directors of Convict Prisons, there being no means of furnishing the information required from the Habitual Criminals Office. I am, sir, your obedient servant,

---

To the Directors of Convict Prisons the querist turned with the following result:—

Office of Directors of Convict Prisons,
44, Parliament Street.

Sir,—I am directed by Major Du Cane to acknowledge the receipt of your letter of the —— instant, and to express his regret that it is not in his power to give you the information you ask for.

1. With regard to —— who you say was hanged at —— you may be able to obtain the particulars you require at the prison there.

2. There are no means of giving you the information respecting convicts sent from —— in this office, but if you apply at the Home Office

you might get it, though it is doubtful whether it could be furnished.

I am, sir, your obedient servant,

More perfectly frank and courteous servants the public could not possess. But information, alas! of this the public is as nearly destitute as though it had not the remotest bearing upon any department of national weal:

Surely it is a matter of no mean importance that the most exact and complete information should be possessed as to the origin and history of convict lives.

Had one desired to obtain information on the history and origin of a newt, particulars of every stage of development from its embryo to its perfection would have been ample and to hand. Science, indeed, has bestowed immense pains on how, by what stages and means, a long-legged sheep becomes a short-legged sheep.

To collect information on such momentous questions England's most patient, most powerful understandings have bent themselves. Is it not time that convicts should be made the subjects of a like exact science? After all, even in his most dreadful form, "the proper study of mankind is man."

Is there no ascertainable law by which the genus man developes this most hideous form? Is there no origin of convict species? The question needs answering. The country has no data. The field is an unexplored mystery. Through centuries has it awaited its turn for research. From the plastic being in the cradle, year by year, have been coming up thousands of this most fearful variety of human life. By what forces? Are they natural, or are they artificial?

Might it not be advantageous to the powerful people who rule the convict-kingdoms, carefully to collect and investigate all the events and conditions through which the melancholy subjects have passed? The whole convict system may, after all, be the price of ignorance—a high price, even to a wealthy land. Ought not knowledge to be obtained? Since everywhere embryo convicts are being prepared—since forces which of old, fated to this dreadful variety of men, are in mysterious and ceaseless operation, can knowledge be a matter of indifference, at least, to their unconscious, perhaps helpless victims?

Meanwhile, it is my own opinion that the legal agencies at work on the rough, heedless boy, are hounding through courts and gaols to Portland and Tasmania, as the inhabitants of Kolonbeng hound wild animals through the converging sides of the hopo, until at its furthest end, through the narrow opening, the goaded, maddened beasts leap into the fatal pit. Following the lines of his fate as fixed by the stern discipline and bad name of prison, so far as unofficial eyes may follow, they all converge towards outlaw's life and an outlaw's doom! Save only as he may leap the hedge, or find some gap in it—as the door of a reformatory or a place on the sea—there is but one end. Once in the hopo of Juvenile Criminal Law, and the bitter fate is a Portland or Tasmania pit.

That these impressions are right, facts cannot be adduced. It may not be mere impertinence, however, to express the opinion, since in its truth every one with whom I have conversed, who has had a right to speak—parent, police authority, gaol governor—has in the main agreed.

Let it not be supposed that these opinions argue against punishment. Given public offence, and public correction ought to follow. By wise correction the public lays the corrected under obligation quite as truly as it promotes social well-being. But where lies the reason for the present wide departure from every ordinary mode of administration? If a babe is left to the public to feed, for good and evident reasons it feeds on principles borrowed from baby-feeding in the domestic kingdom. Why then not follow the analogy when a naughty boy falls to the public to correct, and correct on principles borrowed from naughty-boy correction in the domestic kingdom?

In every grade of life, in weak moments hot blood will be hasty, idle hands mischievous. The expression of juvenile emotions may be coarser in Whitechapel than in Belgravia; but, on the whole, there is a wonderful parallel. Why then should the difference in the instrument of correction be so vast? If the public stands *in loco parentis* to the delinquent of the street, why should it use means of correction which not the most fiendish parent under heaven would adopt?

To treat a child for a single, perchance exceptional, deed, done under strong temptation, with punishment hour-by-hour, day-by-day, week-by-week, a month, it may be two, may be six months through, is—apart altogether from the life-long brand you put upon him—worthy only of barbarians and savages!

Would you but reasonably correct the badness of the bad, other advantages would arise than the mere stoppage of that dooming work in which the nation appears to be now unconsciously engaged. The more christian portion of the community would be protected from depredations as they now are not. Forced on the one hand to suffer from children's naughtiness without redress or, on the other, to chastise through the law, it not seldom happens that calm, sensible, and humane men prefer to suffer without redress. Widely viewed, this may turn out to be only a less perilous course to the offender than the more certainly perilous alternative of law. Any way, there is a widely diffused idea amongst such citizens that an appeal to law might hazard their youthful victim's character, chances, and life-long destiny.

But veritable Shylocks there are, whose revenge is such as no appeals can assuage, to whom even proved injustice to a child, to a naughty child, is a mere peccadillo—men who are content if they can seize and punish—these eagerly seek your aid. It is to such citizens you build your juvenile cells and carry on your sacrificial work!

Surely the horror bestowed on the man who sells arm and dagger to do a bloody work might not be unfairly bestowed on the state which stands daily offering her gaol-service to every citizen who has the heart to ask it. Is not guiltier the callousness which offers than the selfishness which accepts?

Let a nation carry on a service like that and in what ought it to end? This question at least is not without an answer.

CHAPTER IV.

A NEW TRIBUNAL.—CORRECTION WITHOUT RUIN.

CAN there be any doubt that justice towards our juvenile offenders is seriously perverted through the want of a suitable tribunal of judgment?

Some seven thousand children are brought before the magistrates of London in a single year. The stake is sufficiently serious to demand careful attention.

Our convict prisons, it is believed by persons who at once have authority to speak and lack the liberty to do so, are supplied with a large proportion of their inmates from the juvenile victims of fatally unsuitable proceedings of law.

Little know the general public of what is done with juvenile offenders. Strangers to lock-ups, police-courts, laws and gaols, and with perhaps a vague idea that the whole apparatus of crime is necessary to the theoretic order of the state, they know nothing of actual processes and results; yet the public are entirely responsible.

Did you ever consider that big and little offenders are passed through the same course of law; that a child of nine hears the bolt lock him in the same station cell, is bewildered by the same "so help you God," is handled by the same gigantic officials, and stands, or surely is held up, in the same dock, and looks upon the same solemn deputy of the Crown as a murderer!

At the risk of being common-place to the few, I will illustrate what you are doing with naughty children, on whom somebody has the heart to demand the judgment of your law.

On the charge of damaging a fence, a boy of fourteen is given into the hands of your agent, the police. Observe the hour—half-past two in the afternoon. By way of beginning, amid a crowd of the street, he is dragged by the collar of his coat to the police-station by one not too apt to treat rough children of the street with more than about one-half the courtesy ordinarily extended to a dog. There, as though already guilty, he is locked in the station cell. It is winter—without fire, without bed, without food, under a sleepless guard, he is kept through the night until next morning. At ten o'clock, between two policemen, he is marched from his cell to a big, black, four-wheeled van, bearing the initials "V. R."—the very van in which you convey criminals condemned to be hanged. In the van, he is locked in one of its compartments in charge of a turnkey. Drawn by state horses, driven and guarded by state officers, he is conveyed to the court house.

At the Court House he is landed in the common cell with that day's delivery of big and little criminals awaiting their trial. Two are boys, and like our victim, new captives; two are thieves on their second or third arrest, and one is under charge of manslaughter. Here he is kept until four o'clock in the afternoon. At half-past three—precisely twenty-five hours after he was taken into custody, food is given. I pause here to observe that this is the treatment of a child! still unconvicted! A pretty commentary surely on a certain proud English aphorism.

At four o'clock, he is led into court, the trial is opened, the oath administered, the book kissed, and thereupon

THE CLERK reads the charge.

MAGISTRATE: "What have you to say for yourself?"

BOY: "I didn't damage any fence. I don't

know anything about it Sir, I was in the field throwing stones at birds."

THE ACCUSER, from the witness-box, states that many depredations have been done on the fence, gives an estimate of his master's loss, declares that depredations were believed to have been done by boys, that he had been watching for some days and would swear he saw the prisoner breaking it.

POLICEMAN (from the same box) gives the bench the exact time, place, and mode of capture. The lad, pursued by his accuser, was caught in the very act of flying from the field in which the fence was situated.

DETECTIVE: (from the same box) "I have against the prisoner a previous charge of stealing iron from the river side"—

BOY, startled at the statement, forgetting himself, interrupts the detective. "It is not true, Sir, I never was—"

POLICE OFFICER: (at the boy's side) "Silence;" accompanied by a grip of his arm.

DETECTIVE continues, " This was on the —— day of ——, before your honour. The conviction was twenty-one days with labour." No proof of personal identity was asked.

MAGISTRATE : " Have you anything else to say ? "

BOY : " It wasn't me. I'm sure I never was in prison. I never stole any iron, there's other boys named —— besides me.

MAGISTRATE : " You must go to prison for one month with hard labour."

The trial occupied four minutes and a half.

That night the boy lodged in gaol. In due course you informed his parents of your conduct. They received the following circular :—

—— Prison.

The Governor of —— Gaol, begs to inform —— that ——, who is confined in this Prison, for damaging two hurdles, and states he is his son, will be discharged from his imprisonment on the —— day of —— at —— o'clock in the morning unless the Governor is informed that he wishes him detained until a later hour.

The Railway Fare for the prisoner's return home may be sent in a letter addressed to the prisoner.

Let whosoever loves fair play weigh the facts. The child had been in your custody nearly twenty-six hours; unwashed, almost unfed, having spent a night on bare boards, with feelings of unusual calmness he was introduced into the formal, yet surely confounding, proceedings of court. There he hears against him accuser, policeman, detective; and alone, a policeman's hand upon his shoulder, he is asked to reply to the evidence—evidence which he has for the first time but just heard. Try to imagine the feelings of a juvenile, fostered by twenty-four hours of a cell, translated to the dock, pushed in a few minutes through legal formalities! How little common-sense must there be in the man who dreams thus to come at truth. Would not the juvenile who in such regions could repress his feelings, arrange his facts, construct his defence, be an embryo Burke?

To the many questions started by the youngster's simple denial of his accuser's and the detective's charges, the Court can, of course, attach but little weight. Indeed, *Cui bono?* Everybody knows, and not least of all a stipendiary, that boys will do mischief and then deny it. Amid the crowd and pressure of graver cases these trifling affairs at the hands of the fairest of men can receive only a rough and ready handling.

Two hundred and fifty dozen children a-year are in like fashion pushed on through London courts alone from street to gaol.

Is there no juster course? Is it possible that delinquents can find their right place through ways so strangely absurd? In the name of child and country is there not need of reform?

The standards of law by which judgment is given are not less unsatisfactory.

If you would do fairly by the culprit, know something of the world beyond villa and garden, rail and business. Imagine yourself in a nest of narrow streets of dingy tumble-down dwellings, through which innumerable narrow passages are burrowed into innumerable courts and alleys and yards, a very labyrinth of confusion to the uninitiated, where the population abound; big and little everywhere, layer upon layer, below ground and above ground; below ground a layer in a cellar, above ground layers piled up three, sometimes four floors deep, a very warren of life. Entering an ordinary room at midnight, you would find a solution of what appeared to you an impossibility, the alleged number of the population of this small area, and a solution of some things besides. A few families afford the luxury of two rooms. The rest marry, eat, breed, and die in one and the same. With daylight the young of these living layers above and below ground, perforce of space turn into the streets. The bigger boys clear off; some to jobs, some to loaf about; some look savage, not a few have seen the inside of a gaol. Children swarm on the doorsteps—children nursing children, children fighting with children, children shouting to children, children delighting children, children everywhere. If a box-organ should be grinding, they will dance till a policeman comes, then they will scutter away.

These wild and aimless humanities with few exceptions have the ordinary drab and dreary look; not even the youngest cheek wears the bloom of childhood. Matted heads, pinched faces, and wistful-looking eyes prevail. The clothes of not a few expose their spindle limbs to pity; a sufficient number of them to attract attention seem to be suffering in the shape of sores on or about the chin from want, or vice, or both, in its third or fourth generation.

If you should go when times are bad, you

will find men lounging about the streets; if when times are good, one half of them mooning or rioting in beershops; and whenever you go you will find women, arms akimbo, lolling against the door-posts,—all that is left of them, a body enfeebled by early motherhood, frequent births, and insufficient food, and a heart chronically relaxed into hopeless languor by the fatal conviction, slowly but surely attained, that early love mocked them with visions of an—to them, at least—impossible home. Occasionally many of them quicken their apathy, lull some memory to sleep, or get rest for to-morrow's work by three pennyworth of gin. On the whole, however, they seem quiet women, willing to let dirt, indecency, and disease have their tyrannical way.

But it must not be supposed that because idle women are to be seen everywhere, that all the women are idle. The earth is not all granite, though granite forms its most prominent points. The house-row has its geology as well as the globe. Three or six women are in each house. Some are washing, some stitching, some are hawking, some are at home; some have gone out, some are in, doing nothing, weeping because they have nothing to do, and some are out, doing nothing, lounging because they 've nothing to do. Here are deposits of sickness, bereavement, dissipation, and despair, lying physically side by side, morally cycles asunder. Yet weight of circumstance presses on all alike.

If you go on a wet day, you will not wonder at resignation to dirt, for then in lakelets and mud the streets and courts are unsurpassed. If it should be night when you go you will not wonder at resignation to indecency; you will find yourself in the very centre of outer darkness. The staircases, which are six housed streets, and some of the courts and yards, not even the moon can light. Here lodge the most melancholy forms of female life, the most prominent peripatetic scamps—the city missionary to the young—and imbruted animalism, married and unmarried, festers unmedicated. Had the place been designed to hedge in, thwart, and conquer every good aspiration of the human soul—to originate and breed up every tendency of human nature to wrong—success could not have been more complete.

Now change the fancy. Sit a judge on a year's batch of little "criminals," the bulk of whom are brought to your bar for justice out of dens fairly outlined in a scene like that.

They have all been locked up for a part day and a night, have not been washed—no unimportant fact in judging of guilt—and probably have only just broken a twenty-four hours' fast. In such condition they stand for trial.

Their ages are as follows :—Twenty-eight are fifteen, eighteen are fourteen, fifteen are thirteen, ten are twelve, thirteen are eleven, four are ten, eight are nine, four are eight, two are seven, and one is six.

Of the merits of the actions with which these

children are charged the law takes no note. The items of judgment in all fairness should have been classified as:

Cases of Folly.
Cases of Naughtiness.
Cases of Stupidity.
Cases of Want.
Cases of Heroism.

But before the law, every child was simply an obnoxious personage who must somehow or other be punished. In each case, the question to be considered was reduced to a minimum,—there is a charge, guilty or not guilty? The law gives its hapless victim no opportunity to plead that when he threw the stone, he was provoked; that when he took the loaf, he had been a week without one regular meal; that when his blows and scuffle broke somebody's nose and watchguard, he was indignant against a cruel wrong. Could not the State adopt some more fair and natural mode of procedure?

Why are these little urchins in her hands? They are there in the first place through their strong childish propensities; in the second place through exercising these propensities in the street, not in a home. The street is the State nursery,—to its delinquents therefore she stands *in loco parentis.*

Would it not be worthy of her position to emancipate her agents from all present criminal laws, to instruct them broadly to consider all circumstances,—youth, natural propensities, temptations, and lot,—to allow all reasonable excuses, to declare, not simply guilty or not guilty of the action charged, but the reasonableness or unreasonableness of the person who makes it, and in the interest of the whole community to pronounce on the expediency or inexpediency of punishment, and of what sort it should be, but in no case to allow imprisonment.

Does the reader exclaim, Impracticable! What time it would consume! The reply is, Time must be consumed.

You have it in your power to say *when;* whether at this age or at that,—with the child or with the man; but this is the extent of your liberty,—you *must* give it. Let your Courts begrudge time to-day, and the victim will wring it from them to-morrow. There is a homely adage about stitches, which is a political principle too. The hours of a judge are a high price to pay for the minutes of a magistrate. Give the street urchin your time, or pray let him alone.

The means by which deed might be distinguished from deed are many.

Three obviously,—

The Stipendiary.

An Auxiliary Jury.

A New and Distinct Tribunal.

Of these, the first is the last.

The Stipendiary! This plan is in the least degree hopeful. Might not the Stipendiary happen to be a tall, rigid man, with a cavity where the bowels should be, and eleven and a half inches from hip to hip? A generous girth is no mean factor in fair play. Or perhaps he might be a bachelor,—crotchety, irritable, and aged to boot. If so, no amount of investigation could inform him. The faculty needed for the comprehension of the case in which he is judge is altogether lacking. Such inquiry would be impossible.

An Auxiliary Jury! This is a better proposal. And why not a jury? Is not life in the scale—life, whose chances are to be taken or preserved? Given the power of a Grand Jury over all charges which on examination proved to be the acts of childish folly, sheer want, or simple stupidity, and one half the cases which swell the Juvenile list would never appear, or appearing, would never be passed into Court, and would thus save the Magistrate's time and the child's good name.

A New and Distinct Tribunal! This is the best device! A tribunal of citizens—men and women—superintendents of Sunday schools, teachers of day schools, if you will,—why not? Citizens whose functions should be magisterial, whose legal qualifications should be their ability to read the living literature of English children, whose Act of Parliament should be their own moral instincts, with the discretionary powers of a domestic *Habeas corpus ad satisfaciendum*,—above all, who had committed and had not forgotten the appetitive and pugnacious follies of youth, and could "Laugh them o'er again."

Cannot some way be devised which should make clear the merits of every act of child-crime, be sensitive to fair play, be alive to the common weal, regard a child as the father of a man, see him in wider, deeper, higher, more lasting relationship than his relationship to some pitiless, pettifogging pastrycook, recklessly indifferent to everything in heaven, earth, and under the earth, but the loss of a two-penny pie!

Is it not time to let the ridiculously big name "Juvenile Crime" drop from our language, and the consequent hideous impersonation, a Juvenile Criminal, vanish from our fancy,—time to relieve the stealing of apples of the tremendous word which law thrusts upon it,—to drop the humbug of the legislative distinctions "Felonious Intent," "Misdemeanour," "Depredation," "Assault with intent to do grievous bodily harm," and all the rest of it?—to talk and act towards a young ragamuffin sensibly, at least as sensibly as we talk and act towards the more fortunate child of our homes? Might we not by a reasonable economy in hateful and degrading names economise in robbery of juvenile chances, in soured spirits, in perverted powers, in ghastly destinies? Is it not possible that by nicer names on the tongue might be achieved ends more just to the child, more loyal to the State?

Does it not occur to you that a hard-and-fast law against children's deeds, which we have thought proper to call crimes, is horribly ridiculous? Imagine, if it be not too absurd, a collier, born and living in the grimy caverns of a coal-pit, judged by some hard-and-fast penal law of cleanliness. Where, then, is the reasonableness of judging a child born in the caverns of a moral coal-pit by a hard-and-fast penal law of virtue? Can the irrational in the physical be rational in the moral? You can never deal fairly with such a child without ungrudging and generous allowance for circumstances—circumstances which he did not make, which he could not altogether nor always resist. Even a man is to a great extent the creature of his place. What then must be a plastic child? He is but a helpless atom of a tremendous mass. He shares the fate of his moral as well as of his physical circumstances. What he would have been as a parlour child, how can he be either in dress or thought? He derives his rough head and rough notions from the world in which he moves.

This legalized procedure to a child is fatal statesmanship! The working of imprisonment on rough humanity can be almost infallibly predicted. Dismal, exasperating, life-long calamity follows by a law as certain as the law of sunset and night, resulting in consequences not to the youth alone, but to the mass of unfortunate humanity whom he is ungaoled to contaminate. And what is usually the peculiar constitution you are dooming with a life-long doom? Not the feeble, small, mean-souled,—these stand your discipline without much change,—it is the fervid, wit-force, heart-force, generous-to-everybody-but-to-himself sort of boy that you snare in your gins, whose spirits you poison, all whose chances, whose life and character you prematurely and permanently destroy, whose energies you turn to his own and to his country's curse. And all for what!

True, Blackstone might stop his ears at the following lines, but what of that? Can Blackstone create or annul the law of the nature of things? And is not that law one for Rulers of nations and rulers of households?

He who checks a child in terror,
Stops its play, or stills its song,
Not alone commits an error,
But a grievous moral wrong.

Then give it play, and never fear it,
Active life is not defect;
Never, never break its spirit,
Curb it only to direct.

Would you stop the flowing river?
Think you it would cease to flow?
Onward it must go for ever,
Better teach it where to go.

In the 3000 children which in one year you swept from the metropolis into gaols, you grossly disobeyed this common-sense teaching,—you ruled in face of fixed, forbidding moral laws. Of what avail will it be that you have Blackstone to back you when, as surely they must, those fixed moral laws arise to judgment?—laws which are no respecters of either parchments or persons, and exact to the uttermost farthing.

This is an awful subject. In the light of two

or three cases that you well knew, did you ever query what might have been the man of the hulks had you not resentfully plundered boyhood's chances of labour in return for the boylike plunder of plums or for the manful upholding of a mother's rights? Thanks to the grand fairness of the Maker of all things, wrong cannot be sown to ragged wretches, even by Imperial hand, without somewhere wrong being reaped. In that herd of diabolised humanity at Portland the State may find some awful proof.

Cannot you devise ways and means of correcting street urchins' wrong deeds less terribly disastrous?

On the merits of the case, the embryo convict might have turned out to be a hero. Fifteen years ago he fought; perchance his blows drew blood, yet he was inspired not by malice, but by love; struggled not with weakness, but with power; he drove from the shoulder not against justice but against injustice,—not for himself, but for another.

The performances of his heroism may have been a coarse, bungling affair, but it was heroism, and the maudlin moralism which would justify casting him into prison would justify the like to glorious Amyas Leigh, and send to the hulks the manful young Jewish Lawgiver himself. Is it morality at all? Is it not maudling bigotry? Any way, is it not bad statesmanship?

Why does not the aggrieved street lad resort to constitutional means of redress? inquires some peace-loving reader. What knows he of constitutional redress? Given a parish "solicitor," as there is a parish doctor, and the case might have been different. He knows there is a doctor; he has sometimes been for one. Perhaps he has heard the name solicitor, but in all their troubles he has never been for him, nor does he know any other person in his court who has. Guardians have dressed their wounds, but magistrates have never redressed their wrongs. But, were the law within his reach, have you ever for a moment considered with what sentiments he must regard it? What can he possibly know of law, except through what he sees, feels, and understands? His rude heart goes out, as refined hearts go out, after a hero, and the lad in whom he finds his hero,—the lad with the noblest qualities of which he knows, —"the law" is almost sure to gaol. It is the Nero, martyring the saints of his church. With his knowledge of its operations, respect would be impossible, save to sympathies in the lowest stage of barbarism. He must be an ultra Carlylist,—worship power; a fly-wheel in a factory which "takes up" every hapless wretch who gets the rag of his jacket into its teeth. In his sphere of observation, limited it is granted, —such is law: a fly-wheel in the factory of the State, taking up in its clutches—made indeed to take up in its clutches—the like of him, who unwittingly get too near, and to fling them round and round a treadmill.

To the sight of his "chum" led off to gaol,

led off possibly with the brutal rudeness of his captor—this depends on the *personnel* of the man on duty—he may be resigned, as to hard fate, or he may, and if the blood course fast about his heart he must, chafe against the wrong with wild and helpless resentment.

May not the time have come to abandon altogether the practice of juvenile imprisonment? Have we not long enough transformed the errors of momentary ignorance and selfishness into habits and dispositions of a life! Should we not come nearer to the facts of the case if we were henceforth to assume that between the delinquent lad and the average of any dozen lads to be met in an ordinary thoroughfare there is, on the whole, not a pin to choose. The rough fellow in custody may have hotter blood, stronger muscled heart, more enterprise, less to eat or less to do than they; but he is neither better nor worse.

Have we not long enough wrought bad

transformations on the strength of the untutored young, inspired them with darker genii and worsted all their chances? Have we not long enough by Reformatory—the proper historical complement of the gaol—tried to rekindle a hope we had ourselves quenched, to tame a spirit we had already maddened? Have we not long enough forgotten that the fortunes of our little citizen, of the family of which he is a child, of the family of which he is potentially a father, depend on his ability to get work. Have we not long enough handcuffed him, blind to the fact that the handcuff meant no work, that in a deep sense we handcuffed him for life; that his own necessities, the necessities of his younger brothers and sisters, and the necessities of his potential children, all remain; that practically we have laid the morals of a generation and the taxes of a kingdom under tribute?

Alter our present unjust, irrational, impolitic mode of procedure, we must, if we are ever to evolve from England's neglected and erring child a better thing than the aimless loafer or demoniac monster which at much cost of gold and time we are evolving to-day.

PART II.—INOCCUPATION.

CHAPTER I.

WILLING TO WORK—NO CHANCE.

CAN the rough, wild energy of the street be utilized?

The question begins to stand out in a promising twilight!

Business men who have studied the matter from the standpoint of personal experiment, eminently those who have done so in some fine, perchance exceptionally promising specimen, taken direct from the streets, hold a strong and almost unanimous opinion. They reaped only trouble for their pains. In their judgment, the theoretically possible becomes the practically impossible, and in committees, on platforms, in parliament, they pronounce accordingly.

Did the judge in this matter ever fairly consider the perilous conditions under which ordinarily, at least, perhaps in their own case, the experiment is made?

The following incidents are of rough noble-natured lads, driven back in their upward struggle. Possibly they may shed a ray into the dawn which breaks upon the whereabouts of the uncommercialised lad in this world of commerce, and penetrate to the reason why the difficulties he has to contend with so often prove fatal.

Rigged out in a new blouse and cap, with clean patched trousers and polished patched boots, one of the brightest-faced little fellows in London commenced a promising career as errand-boy to an ironmonger. The conceit at his appearance, as he in company with the gentleman who had befriended him left a second-hand clothier's shop, the satisfied sense of superiority he felt in his new "rigging," the smiles with which he looked first on himself, then on his friend, and indeed on everybody and on everything along the way to the shop where he was to be in a "place," and most of all on the bright future which that place was opening to his modest ambition, made the friend fully as happy as the lad.

* * * * * *

In the dusk of a summer evening, through a dark passage, up four flights of dark stairs, in what had been a century ago a handsome house —now let out to some dozen or fifteen families —in a large, low room, the boy's friend found the boy's mother seated in a rocking-chair, wearing spectacles, working at the button-holes of a waistcoat, with face and waistcoat close together, and both close to a lighted paraffin lamp, furnished with a shade extemporised out of a newspaper. The door was opened by pulling a string which communicated through a hole with a latch on the other side. The room was entered without its being perceived that the boy had with him a stranger. At the announcement, "Mother, here's a gentleman as wants me for a place," the woman instantly put down her work, took off her glasses, and lifted away the paper shade which intensified light on the work, but left the rest of the room in the mysterious darkness of dusk. Pointing to her feet, which were of enormous size and swathed in cloths, she apologised for not rising. "I have not seen the righteous forsaken, nor his seed begging bread," could never have been written by one who had witnessed the struggles of that afflicted woman through the eleven years of her widowhood. Gout, rheumatism, and disease of the eyes seemed to have taken malicious delight in baffling all attempts to win bread for herself and her three children. Her tailors' work was very irregular, and her ability to do the little that she got was more irregular still. She would struggle through a job in an agony; and when tolerably well, could not do more than one shilling's worth in her sixteen-hour day. Ofttimes the sharpness of the agony rendered work altogether impossible. Then days and nights were spent in moaning. At such times this crossing-boy was the family's only support. To his translation to the shop the woman gave her most grateful consent.

* * * * * *

"No, sir, I cannot continue him. I am very sorry, *very sorry* INDEED, but I cannot go on with him; he must leave. And the men, too, they won't have him, that's the long and short of it. I'm sorry, but I can't help it, sir. I fear such lads are hopeless."

Such was the verdict of the master pronounced upon the errand-boy, four weeks after the brave little fellow had entered on his new service, with much irritation and emphasis, to the friend who had introduced him. The fourth and last week's wage was paid, and, in company with his friend; the broken-hearted lad went home.

The doom had come about thus. The lad, not many days after his admission to the situation, had been sent out with a watering-can. When happy, he was prone to whistle or sing, and as he whistled or sang, nothing was more natural to him than to beat time with whatever might be in his hand, and on whatever might be within reach. Whistling as he went along, this happy little thoughtless soul, as a sort of musical accompaniment, drummed the bottom of his can on the top of a row of palisadings which combined the doubly-unfortunate circumstances of being of height low enough to admit of such a performance, and of having spear-headed tops, sharp enough to make a serious impression on the bottom of a can. The can was duly delivered at the house of its owner.

Scarcely had the boy returned to the shop when the servant-maid brought back the can, with the angry announcement that the bottom was "a perfect sieve." The boy, totally innocent of what he had done, was called. The workman who had bottomed the can was called too, and he with the maid and the master joined in an excited outburst of charges and questions, which speedily reduced the little fellow to tears.

"What did you do it with, you young monkey, what did you do it with?" said the maid.

"I didn't do it with nothing," sobbed the confounded boy.

"Come, now, no more of your lies; you've done it, and you know you've done it, you mischievous young varmint, you," said a gross, selfish-looking workman, seizing the lad by the collar.

"I didn't do nothing, I'm sure I didn't," replied the now utterly-terrified boy.

"Are you sure it came to you like this?" said the master, looking first at the can-bottom and then at the maid.

"Sure! If I was to die this minute, I'm sure and certain."

The company then dispersed; the workman to the workshop, the maid to her home, the master and boy to the counting-house.

"Come, my boy," said the master gently, when they were alone, "come, my boy, don't you remember? Think again. Tell me the truth, I won't punish you."

Whether the lad cried, or laughed, or sang, his feelings always broke all over him like a wave; his sorrow did not just touch a muscle here and there, it desolated his soul, it shook him to the very core. This entireness of sorrow had moved the master with compassion.

"I've been a-thinking, sir, may be it was them railings, sir. I touched it a bit on the railings, sir."

The master's countenance became more stern; he saw at once how the can had been perforated, and charged the boy with mischief, deliberate mischief; for what else could it be? All the presumptions were, of course, against such lads; this confession confirmed them.

Had the play of the master's feeling been freer and larger, he would have pitched upon some more generous solution than deliberate mischief; or had the boy been cultivated enough to have understood, and explained himself, he would have put himself beyond such a suspicion; but neither of these conditions existed, and the true key of the problem was missing—viz., understanding the boy. Consequently, the master went home to reply to his his wife's

"What's the matter?"

"Why, that boy you are so taken with has deceived me. He's a little hypocrite, I fear." And the boy went home to reply to his mother's

"What's the matter?"

"Why, they say, mother, as I'm a liar, and I've spoilt a can on purpose."

* * * * * *

A week had only just gone when the boy's enthusiastic nature brought him into further trouble. As he took home a porcelain jug wrapped in paper, he observed two dogs fighting, or, to use his own language, "a dastard big dog a-worrying a little un." He rushed to the rescue, kicked the worrier, but it did not desist; then, absorbed entirely in his kind work, he "fetched it a rattler" on its head with the jug; there was a crash, not, however, from the dog's skull, but from the boy's parcel.

He dare not go back to the shop. At his friend's house he declared, in a way that would have moved a stone, "It's no use, they'll not have me no more."

The lad's nature was a brave and beautiful nature, but it was entirely untrained. Persuaded that the price of its training was a little patience and a little money, his friend paid for the jug, as he had previously paid for the can. His strong faith in the lad's possibilities was strengthened by the master's expression, after a catalogue of his faults, "He seemed to be looking up a bit after that can affair."

"Do be patient with him a little longer,"

said the boy's friend to the foreman of the smith-shop, whom the boy had to assist when not out on errands, and to whom the master had referred him as the man with whom the case chiefly rested—a gross, supercilious, selfish-looking man, of some sixteen stones' weight.

"Well," the smith replied, "parsoning's a parson's trade, it ain't ours; bisnis is bisnis; if he stops here somebody'll be smashing his head."

The friend spoke to him of the boy's mother, of her widowhood, of her sufferings, of her ill-paid work, of her three children, of the blessings of God on those who considered the poor, of the boy's anxiety to "do," of the master's observation of improvement, of the pleasure there would be in the reflection that, by his patience with the lad, he might indirectly help in lighting up a bereaved family and a distressed home, to which he replied, seizing his file and resuming his work, "He's a lying young lout."

Such was the man on whose temper and will the destiny of the boy mainly rested, and he is a sample of British workmen, on whose temper and will depends the destiny of many a little untrained yet earnest struggler. But should you Christianise your English workmen, it is not likely even then that for our hero and all his kith and kin, the ordinary arrangements of business will furnish a way up from idleness to labour.

Doubtless, to the selfish unsympathetic animalism of the smith, there are exceptions, many and illustrious. But under such favourable circumstances, a vital something would be wanting, ere with any show of reason it could be fairly expected that the struggles of lads who have alike the material and the desire to rise above the vagabond's life will be generally crowned with success.

Another fatal defect in the ordinary external conditions under which the attempt to civilize and commercialise raw, wild lads from the

London brick and mortar jungles is made, stands out in the following by no means exceptional fact. The subject was a more twinkling, springy, rushing little fellow than the unfortunate young amateur smith. His antecedent history is given, because it renders domestication more probable.

"What's the matter, Johnny?" said the lady of a house to a quick, eager-looking boy of an old fifteen. The boy is seated with the servants in a comfortable Christian home. It is Sunday evening, the family have gathered for worship, they are singing an evening hymn. Suddenly the usually happy and careless boy is in tears—a chord of memory has been touched.

"We did this when mother was alive," replied the boy, sobbing.

Fourteen years before, a young married couple came up from the country to seek their livelihood in the great city—the great mocking city! They were of the middle class, had a little money, a little health, and an excellent character. The husband was a builder, the wife was a mother, and our hero was her child.

Ten slow, bitter years gone, and there might be seen a crowd gathered round the door of a small house in a narrow street in ——. It had gathered to witness the last scene in the lives of the same couple. To-day they are to be conveyed in the same van, under the care of the same official, to the same hospital. From that hospital, a few days later, they were carried to the same grave.

In the room from which the van conveyed the stricken husband and wife there was left a little furniture and a boy-child.

When it was known by the woman of the house that her lodgers would return no more, she offered the child four pounds ten for his parents' furniture—all that remained of a once comfortable home. The child took the money, and at nine years of age started life alone in London with four pounds ten in his pocket!

Hitherto he had been the object of refined love. When his parents were well-to-do, and when they had been reduced to extremest poverty, his portion of home's food, and bright and tender care had been the portion of an only child. The face which in baby-days lay in a snug cot of muslin and ribbon and down, was kissed, perhaps, more tenderly—certainly as tenderly—when, at nine years of age, he slept on a father's empty tool-box, made bed-like by a mother's frock.

He found his way to a coffee-house, in the window of which hung the notice, "Beds." He went in, showed the landlady all his money, and asked if he might live there. She consented, and there he began his lonely life. His money, however, was soon all gone, and then he was initiated into the business of buying and selling newspapers. Through lighter clothing, scantier food, rain and cold, he was often ill. At such times he was allowed to go into debt, but when he left his sick bed the little fellow had to work very hard through long hours, in all weathers, to make up his arrears. And all this before he was ten years old!

For four long years the orphan dragged on his solitary existence in London streets. His star-eyed, delicate face became familiar to the officers of the State, but the State does not help a homeless child until he has been injured by neglect. Would he but steal a lady's watch, the State would force on him a cook, a schoolmaster, a little library, a clergyman, a seat at church, and instruction in some art by which he could make a living. Would he but partially succumb to the cruel—almost resistless—temptations of the street, and become only the crony of thieves—not a great demand after all—the State would contribute towards six years' board and lodgings in a certified school. Would his fragile frame but sink under privation, and one of his many sicknesses end in death, the State would find him a shroud and a grave. This eminently stupid little fellow would not accept any of these pleasant alternatives, and to help before disaster to body or soul occurred would be to violate the fundamental principle of a free government. So the State stood by, and awaited the issue of this little fellow's miserable, and—to the imperial watcher—disgraceful struggle for life.

Finally there came the "tide" in his affairs.

It is the evening of an October day. He has been taught to sing, and has set out to make his first public effort. The police come down upon him, and that night the little fellow spends in the lock-up!

Inside the doors past which he sang men and women were being poisoned and damned by the licence of the British people. Outside, the same sovereign authority took into custody an orphan-boy for seeking his livelihood by a song and a hat!

Next morning the stipendiary dismissed his cases with ease, until our hero stood in the dock. The boy's face was open, pale, pure, and sad, his carriage erect, his manner quick, almost refined, his clothes patched but not torn, his person thin, but fastidiously clean. The police could bear no evil testimony except the crime of last night. Still, practically, the law left no alternative but prison or reformatory. Had he succumbed to the temptation to beg at an earlier period in his history, he might have gone to the milder discipline of an Industrial School. But he has stood out too long. He is six days too late, and for the firm stand he had made the sterner penalties of prison or reformatory was the State's reward. Prison! as well send an angel to prison.

Reformatory! What was there in a boy who had passed from nine to past fourteen through the fiery furnace of an independent street life, and to whom the keen-scented policeman bore testimony that it had not left on him so much as the smell of fire, to need the discipline of a reformatory?

The case was perplexing. The boy was remanded until the morrow.

The transfer from the police-court to the Christian household had come about thus:—The day after the "trial" the chief journal reported the dilemma of the magistrate; a merchant friend of the present writer, residing some miles away from the court, read it, and appeared in the court to request that his home might be the prison, his service the penalty. The magistrate, by some generous evasion of the law, gladly consented to the request.

The boy became a willing captive. His wish was to be civilized. He was honest, he was earnest. He set his face to his new duties, and was proud of his new dignity.. He bravely fought against formidable tendencies of tongue and hand, and exasperating obstacles raised by the unsympathetic character of the men with whom he worked, and made some evident progress. In the office he began to win confidence, in the kitchen to become the object of affec tion. In the evenings he improved his already tolerable education; in the savings-bank he laid up his earnings, and seemed likely enough to fall into a home-life.

Suddenly he was gone!

Why gone? Not a shilling, not a stamp, not a rag had he taken. With such facts, a healthy mind will not find it difficult to divine the answer. A tenth-time repeated blunder, a tenth-time repeated censure, a weak, despairing moment, an illusive memory, an open door! That is the history of the exit, and the history of hundreds of like exits. Ceaseless effort wearies, inevitable failures depress, memory of vanished freedom tempts, an open door conquers.

And where is reason for surprise?

Conceive, if you can, the past condition of the class of boy with which you are dealing. Obedient to his only authority—a set of raw impulses—he has rushed hither and thither without any other reason than that he just thought that he would. In his "home," things have gone along in a confused huddle, always following a sort of blind chance ; and the street troop, into which he and his like organized, moved in a wild sort of fashion not unlike the gregarious animals of a desert. His very order has been disorder, his harmony confusion.

Imagine the true child of such a life suddenly entering into a new world—a world where he has to embrace a new ideal of life, fall under well-considered rule, repress his strongest and most complex propensities, reverse a thousand and one habitual and involuntary actions, and what is more evident than that to such a child, at first, small success and large failure are inevitable.

That nature must indeed be far above, if not far below, the nature of ordinary beings, which could long continue in such a world without collapse somewhere. Then, with the collapse, what more natural, nay inevitable, than the gravest doubts in the mind alike of the hapless adventurer, and of his possibly not over-patient master, or not over-refined superintending workman, whether anything can be made of such material.

Hardly has he entered upon his new dignity before he finds what is in store for him; failure, oft-repeated failure. Then when failure comes, unfortunately, earnestness of purpose does not help; on the contrary, the more intense the lad's upward desire, the more intense the consequent dejection, and the more thoroughly his "place" is a place of "bisnis," the more perilous does such dejection become. The tongues of busy men are always charged with lightnings for "hands" who are in their way; and what more likely than that street lads should be in the way, and kicks and curses do not cheer a desponding spirit, nor brace a failing will.

Until the period of volition and struggle is passed, rushingness dropped, method acquired, nature indeed completely reversed, the conditions of a specially adapted institution are absolute to start our "Arabs" in industrial life. The intuitions of the domesticated lad, however poor, are the natural foundations of a methodical, working life; but the intuitions of the free child of the streets, are precisely the reverse. What is spontaneous to the one is forced to the other—forced by resolve, made and remade and backed by long wearying effort. In days he has to do and undo the work of years. He has to drop habits which others never formed, and to acquire, *ab initio*, what others never lacked.

For such a battle do your ordinary business places afford a fair field? Their conditions fairly weighed, success not failure is the curiosity.

Was not the smith right after all? Did he not cut into the heart of the matter, and lay bare the whole difficulty when he said, "Bisnis is bisnis." Your City cab is not the proper place in which to break a fresh filly. How then can you expect ordinary commercial life to supply the conditions in which to "break" the street-made lad?

Ten thousand such lads await their chance. There is absolutely no provision for them save streets to lounge in. For the workhouse they have as yet too much sinew, for the gaol too much honour, and for the schools too many years!

Surely, Ragged School Union, you at least might direct your funds to their eminent want. Under the happily changed conditions of education, with a Parliament for children, what so worthy of your original purpose? How better can you help the helpless, and please the God you name at your great gatherings? Erect henceforth shops and homes for industrial training. Let them be small, numerous, transitional shops where lads may acquire the habits of the labour market without unreasonable demands—reasonable enough to commercial men, but eminently unreasonable to the half-civilized lad,—homes where discipline would be adjusted to meet inevitable and perilous moods, and the lad who had crossed the rubicon, should always find that somebody else had burnt his ship. Does he not need this? ought you not to give it him?

Thanks-deserving Union, adapt your beneficence to the times! Change your name. By the principles and professions whereof you are the grand monument, by ten thousand lives, pending between labour and the treadmill —honest, willing, eager to be men,—change your name! Announce yourselves henceforth "The LABOUR SCHOOL UNION;" in at once abolishing your "Ragged" name, you might gradually abolish the "ragged rascal" too.

Every penny the generous give you, now spent by you on ordinary day schools is, in London at least, needless. Spend on small unpretentious, transitional Labour schools, and you will merit and win your country's thanks.

Leaders, you are responsible. Commanding the liberality of a vast constituency, yours is the opportunity. Yours the power to obstruct or lead!

CHAPTER II.

EMANCIPATION FOR THE IDLE—COMPULSORY LABOUR.

ONE day a woman died. She was a seamstress. Next day her husband, a lumpish, loafing, drinking fellow, turned his back on his house and child. The child was the only one at home, and a boy.

In a London gaol there is at this time a criminal who has for the fifth time occupied one of its cells. At his first imprisonment he was three weeks short of fifteen, at his last imprisonment he was four weeks over sixteen, and that criminal is none other than our seamstress' son.

The following are the verified particulars of his transmigration from honesty to theft. The day following the one on which his father left him, at threepence per day he found roof and bed, and joined other boys who lodged together and made a pretty fair living by their wits. Some of them had parents living, several had parents dead; whether their parents were living or dead the rest neither knew nor cared, —why should they? Here, too, were three unmarried girls, who also were homeless, and two married women who had husbands at sea, "stands" in Cheapside, and children, inmates of the same house. Self-governed knots of lads from twelve to nineteen infested the neighbourhood, most with nothing to do, the rest with no more than nominal employment. If they did not avoid mischief, the most rigid Pharisee must own no surprise. At all events, getting into gaol had long been regarded as the special accident inseparable from their modes of life.

"Hob-jobbing," to use the vividly descriptive phrase of his class in life, through thirteen months the lad somehow managed to appease, occasionally to satisfy the cravings of nature, and to keep his head under his hired roof; yet, not very wonderful to record, his primeval ideas of theft meanwhile undergoing considerable modification.

"Never wait till you're hungry, that's the way to get the blues," said his eldest companion, the only accredited vicar of the place, when times were looking bad, and our hero seemed to need a friendly councillor. "You never makes a good market on a 'empty belly—that's my sight o' things."

For thirteen months, from like external and internal arguments and facts, our hero had turned away with at first a frown and subsequently a laugh. Days came in which there was a hob-jobber's famine; no horses to hold, no parcels to carry, no money to buy, *ergo* no fish to sell. Such crises often occur, and sorely try the hob-jobber's conscience. There was unusual snow, and then rain, rain, rain. Rent and stomach are in dreadful arrears; another day's rain, and morals or life must go. The fatal rain falls,—why, is a mystery save to the God who sent it. Of course, Mr. Well-fed moralist, than steal it would be better to starve, and go to the martyr's heaven, but how about dying in debt? Heroically might the arrears of the tumultuous stomach be left to run up to bankruptcy, but how about the arrears of lodgings?

While this double problem of existence peremptorily presses for solution, a gentleman, with a cut-of-coat which ought to be made illegal,—which certainly has much to answer for in leading into temptation,—a top-coat with tails and gaping tail-pockets, standing looking into a shop window, feels a sensation which proceeds from contact of his coat tails with something behind. Eyes and hands are quickly on the cause,—it is our hero solving his problem. Being a just man, the owner of the pocket-handkerchief gives his shivering victim in charge. His companions, unaccustomed to excite themselves at such affairs, receive the news of the lad's fate with a kindly apathy, one observing, "Cold fingers an' empty bellies I allars says is clumsy tackle."

Now we are at the feature of the case. In touching the handkerchief, the lad touched the hand that led him to a fair structure, where no hunger is unfed, no ignorance uninstructed, no idleness unemployed.

Among the provisions of the gaol is a labour school, and now the "hob-jobber about" is in the custody of its master. Being already a tolerable reader and writer, the first fruit of his theft was something to do. Three months you instructed him in mat-making, and, but for the place in which you gave your instruction, this systematic occupation might still have started his muscles and morals on some fair way to honourable calling. But, honourable calling! Well knew the governor, and well knew all who have experience in such affairs, that entrance of prison is "bon jour" to all honourable calling. His time of servitude expired. Name bad, will broken, temper soured, and hope—which seldom survives the air of a prison-cell—quenched, you turned him out on the street.

Three weeks gone, he was in your hands again for a precisely similar offence; this time twenty-one days fell to his lot. The probable solution of this lighter penalty being found in the digestibility of the magistrate's previous night's supper,—mercy is not in a disordered liver. For twenty-one days you taught him mat-making.

A third time he returned to gaol, and a third time you taught him mat-making, this time for three months.

A fourth time he was in your hands, a fourth time you taught him mat-making, this time also for three months.

A fifth time he was in your hands, and again you taught him mat-making, and this time also for three months.

Thirteen whole months you compelled attendance at the school of mat-making, thirteen months you paid rates to support the school of mat-making. Every time the pupil did wrong, you gave him more instruction, every time you gave him instruction he repeated his wrong, the price of his tuition was wrong-doing. He committed a theft, and therefore made a mat, he committed another theft, and therefore made another mat!

Whatever mats were made in gaol, thefts and thieves were made abroad. Himself done for, he does for others. How universal is love of fellowship! Soon the tale of his captured disciples reaches half-a-dozen. He is known now as a ringleader of junior outlaws.

Knowing each time that there lay in the nature of things almost a necessity for his return, physical and moral, urgent and well ascertained, when his time was served, you turned him up, each time a better mat-maker, each time more inevitably and notoriously a thief. And now how can you deal with him, except as with your convicts, and give him, in a bayonet-guarded labour-school, penal servitude for life?

Impartially reflect on this drama of the law and the lad, and can you imagine that it was the work of a sane people?

Yet, were not half your convicts made out of similar lads whom you as often and as uselessly instructed? What if you had trained them to labour whilst they had a good name? How many of them bravely held out day by day for months! With how many was failure a begrudged and only half-conscious concession to a deadly *duresse*? How many, had you given them a labour-school outside a gaol, had been respectable artisans, perchance the ornaments and strength of their class? What possible utility can there be in waiting to teach until teaching comes too late, in putting your hands into the public treasury to correct an evil whose *vera causa* you at the same time make more hopelessly fixed and certain? In the name of all the practices and principles and professions of English statesmanship, what soundness can there be in a course whose inseparable result in some of the strongest brained and strongest hearted manhood is a hopeless, maddened, and life-long ruin! If such a deadly fate be justice, is not one tempted to agree with Angelo, that a judge shows "pity" to at least the urchin of the street, who

> "Answering one foul wrong,
> Lives not to act another?"

Than this, is not your tender mercy a gallows, a rope, and the drop?

More comical, less tragical, yet not less instructive, are the following particulars :—

Our hero, a quick-witted, cast-eyed, tall boy of sixteen, returned from gaol less damaged than any of the ex-prisoners it has been my fortune to know. In him a disposition, always easiful and kindly, survived the "six months with hard labour" in an altogether exceptional manner. From the day on which his name was struck off the register of his school, up to the day on which it was inscribed on the register of the gaol, his occupation had been that of all idle boys—"hob-jobbing about." His crime was stealing coals. The very day of imprisonment he was compelled to work, and he needed no compulsion. With a will he stitched at the appointed shoe; if his work was clumsy, it was the fault of muscles dead with idleness; honestly he plied awl and needle, and cast many a thought on the future prosperity of the family. Thirteen weeks gone, he left the gaol and started hopefully on an industrious life. How inevitably mocking his hope, all who know anything of efforts for ex-prisoners' employ too well know, and the victim himself soon learnt.

The hero's home was a single room on the ground-floor in an ordinary tenth-rate street; its inmates were his mother, a hawker, and two brothers, younger than himself, "hob-jobbing" about. Accompanied by his mother, he tried to get work at shoemakers' shops, offered to do it cheap, then he hung in the window, "Shus and Butes mending," innocently resolving that should he get anything to do, he'd try to borrow some tools to do it with; but the fatal "Gaol" kept boots from his house, and him from a shop.

Weigh the facts of the family.

To begin with, how did your favour come into this widow's house? It followed your capture of her son. The people imposed it upon her as the reward of a son's wrongdoing.

Why to one child only has the State taught elements of a trade? Clearly because he has qualified for her instruction, but qualified by a qualification which renders his instruction totally useless.

Why are the two remaining brothers untrained, without motive or master, doomed to loaf about the streets? So far as you are concerned, because, as yet, idleness has not taken from them their good name. Their hands cannot touch your tools till they consent to break your law.

Countless are the illustrations of such legalised, yet surely, stolid stupidity.

Year by year from fifty to sixty thousand London children pass out of elementary schools; of these possibly the half obtain *bonâ fide* occupation; as for the rest—the poorer part—there is nothing for them but the streets, and the highly probable life of a knave or a fool. It is probable that, every day, not less than seventy thousand boys and girls are actually "hob-jobbing about," utterly helpless, until they hob-job into gaols, penitentiaries, reformatories, and industrial schools.

Sometimes it is asserted that the young herds of the street are unoccupied because voluntarily idle, and, by way of proof, an appeal is made to the great want of boys in the mercantile world. If intelligent co-operation with typal units has authority to speak foı thousands, it is a complicated tyranny of circumstances which has fixed their destiny. If in the thing supplied there must be at least some correspondence with the thing demanded, the conclusion that, because there are in London ten thousand vacancies for youthful workers, and ten thousand useful *might-be* workers are in the streets, therefore youthful inoccupation is guilty, is as profoundly foolish as it is profoundly false.

Imagine one whose dress, habits, physique, associations are all of the kind common to the typal street child whose parents are dead or living and worthless, or worthy and day-long out struggling for existence; and such children there are, not by tens but by ten thousands, here and there, and everywhere in London from centre to circumference. Add to these personal and social considerations, the stern element of geography;—the peremptory conditions of distance at which the vast proportion live from the great natural centres of commerce; remember that there are no work-children's trains, though there are workmen's trains; weigh fairly their chances of labour, and how can you be surprised that, be the demand for youths what it may, hosts are roaming about, picking up perchance sixpences, and certainly the worst of habits. Of nothing-to-do, tens of thousands of young London citizens are entirely guiltless; yet guilty or guiltless one thing is clear, lazy habits and setting muscles are at once mortgaging their own manhood and, in one way or another, the people's revenue.

What is clearly needed is the establishment of compulsory labour schools, and why should they not be in the street as well as in the gaol?

We English are a wonderful people. Long have we had free, compulsory, and rate supported education for ignorance in the gaol. A similar law for ignorance outside the gaol is a thing of only yesterday. We have actually ceased, but have only just ceased from making picking-a-pocket a legislative *sine quâ non* of a beneficent intellectual State provision.

Does it not strike you that the principle of legislative action on ignorance extended to idleness, would create ways and means by which our new epoch would be far brighter? Let public elementary labour schools be established wherever the character of the population and exigencies of labour require them; let the schools be small, numerous, open at the same hour, and for the same times as day elementary education schools; let them be in no sense penal; let them be open for boys and for girls 13 to 18 years old; let them board, or where possible, in every way more desirable, board out the homeless; let them be adapted to half-timers, regarding the occupation or health of the pupil; let them dovetail with the day-school; let the occupation be varied, and the main aim general development of muscle and skill, and, above all, let attendance be compulsory where there is no reasonable excuse for absence, or other beneficial and regular employ—and the Fates would surely mould our hapless urchins into better citizens.

The principle of such a school is already granted. So far as gaols are concerned, it has long been law. We have extended the principle of compulsory education from the criminal to the non-criminal class, why not extend the principle of compulsory labour in like manner? Why should there not be brought home to every unoccupied boy and girl in London streets the provisions made for their less honest brother in the gaol? Bitterly they need it; in all common fairness let them have it.

What are the net results of labour schools confined to prisons? In our heroes' cases what were they? In one *nil;* a little knowledge of shoemaking without the ghost of a chance to use it. In another mat-making and thief-making, yet more thief-making than mat-making, for thieves breed and mats don't. With such results, is not the science of your law a complete failure? Can a lover of the high ends of justice be other than ashamed of the utter stupidity of your means? What, at its very best, is an English gaol but a clean, bright, well-ventilated, magnificent factory of mats and youthful villany—a palace of blundering economy, wrecking and sending out wreckers? And for the sake of these results the taxpayer is year by year putting his hand into his pocket.

Idleness must be interfered with. At the bottom of all hopes for a bright future lies some scheme of youthful occupation as a part. Ordinary education will do much, but as a matter of fact, is ignorance of the Decalogue the cause of theft; or will ability in rule-of-three appease the cravings of hunger, or the history of the Norman Conquest nullify the temptation of pocket-handkerchiefs; or a graceful handwriting alter the forces of home, the misfortune of a profligate father or straitened mother, or bring back parents who lie among the helpless dead? Will a certificate from Her Majesty's Inspector cause the stomach not to abhor a vacuum, or suspend the law about Satan and "mischief still for idle hands to do", or simplify the bewildering conditions of London poor life? Can education, in short, work moral and physical miracles? Is it not well for the educationally sanguine to know that the hopes of those who have authority to speak, at least on the crime-producing aspect of neglecting the young, rest not solely, not chiefly on the day school? At the bottom of them all lies some large scheme of youthful occupation.

An appeal might be made to the occupation

column of the gaol register in proof of the comparatively small influence which occupation exerts on juvenile crime. Such an appeal would be as superficial as the proposition it supported would be false. Of what avail to the lad who has been six weeks idle is the fact that when he can get anything to do he is a "labourer?" Or how can it serve a boy who lounges about from every Monday morning to every Saturday night, that on Saturday nights he is an "errand-boy?" Something more must be known of the case than the gaol register can disclose, or the connection of inoccupation and crime can never be judged fairly.

Interference to be efficient must be State interference. Suitable and sufficient provision must be made wherever the normal condition of commerce does not supply it, and attendance at labour must be enforced—at the public school or in the ordinary shop—somewhere the boy must be compelled to labour.

Is not a compulsory labour law rendered

necessary by the character of full half the parents? necessary as a protection to the State? What do the selfish, animalised parents care for the use or abuse of youth, the duties of citizens, the basis of society, the weal of the State? Themselves living from hand to mouth they feel that it is right to turn out their children, regardless of all future consequences, on the chance of their somehow picking up a copper or two. Were not they themselves turned out, and have not *they* got along! To the possibility of his children growing up to be sleepy labourers, beer-house loungers, idle paupers,—what sleepy labourer, beer-house lounger, idle pauper ever gives a thought? And if it could arise on his stolid imagination, why should he be shocked at the vision? His opinion, if opinion he has at all, is that everybody, wife and children, must "fend" for themselves, and take their chance.

Is not such a law necessary to the discharge of State duty to herds of helpless children?

Amid the tangled complications of their lot; under no parental control, the progeny of the hopeless, the thriftless, the reckless, and the helpless poor, the disadvantages of their years, intricacies of business, contrasting distributions of juvenile labour; demand and supply, fluctuations of trade, constant outshifting of population from work-centres,—they are fated for the stone-yard of the Union or the oakum-room of the gaol. Little know they of their gravest dangers, less of their best possibilities, and less still have they power over the harsh, stern circumstances of their birth. To keep alive, and keep clear of the police is the chief aim of their day-by-day life.

Towards the idle the let-alone policy is fortunately impossible. Your police has his eye on him, your relieving officer takes note of him, your neighbours prophesy about him. Whether you ignore his needs or not, you cannot ignore his existence. He insists on some sort of attention to his condition.

He gives rise to rates and grants and votes in poor law, aldermanic, and legislative councils. Of course he is unconscious of all this care, but he must have it: you may say whether it shall be whilst he has muscle and moral, or when both muscle and moral are wasted. You may erect for him a House of Correction, in which the governor, shaking his head, says it is "too late to mend him,"—and for that he'll curse you; or you may erect a new edifice, a labour-school, where, according to your best gaol authorities, he can be saved from becoming a personal ruin and a social scourge, and for that he'll bless you. You may insist on his being a good citizen, or leave him to become at best a lumpish, lazy labourer,—perchance a bad husband, a worse father, and a worst citizen,—a scamp to breed scamps, and leave his progeny a national heritage. If the let-alone policy were a policy fit for the State, fortunately for the chances of a labour-school it is not possible for the State to pursue it.

Compulsory taxation, or Compulsory Labour, this is your one alternative. And where lies the difficulty in the way of Compulsory Labour? Is it objected that Compulsory Labour would interfere with parental liberty? Then why not?

The State will not, indeed cannot, leave me at liberty to allow the effects of idleness; why should it leave anybody else at liberty to allow the cause? I must pay to dam up the horrid stream. Why should some other person be allowed to open the horrid spring? Surely the money spent in protecting society from the tremendous consequences of neglected youth would be better spent in protecting society from their tremendous causes. Up to thirteen years of age, does not the State already exercise her control. With what consistency can the man who justifies control over action up to thirteen object to wise and beneficent control after thirteen? If up to thirteen is the time for intellectual education, is not beyond thirteen the time for labour-education? Is not the labour history of a boy as great a factor in the welfare of the State as his educational history? Surely the expediency of control during one of the two formative stages of citizen life applies with equal force to the other formative stage? Is your hand on education because education makes men? Does not labour make men? Or is it because education makes the State? Does not labour make the State? Then why must the State take her hand off juvenile citizens at their exit from the day schools? Why, if expedient, may it not continue its control, and require attendance at a public elementary labour-school?

Until yesterday, compulsory education was the monopoly of the prison. Stealing a pocket-handkerchief brought down a raid of the State on ignorance. To-day compulsory labour is still the monopoly of the prison. In some of your prisons, you have teachers half employed and factories half idle, because your British youth are too fastidious to go to use them.

Doubtless compulsory education was good for inmates of gaol; by it, may be, some young Englishmen have learnt to read and write who had no chance until they came under its beneficent operation. Equally doubtless is it that the lack of compulsory education was a bad thing for youth outside the gaol. Countless evils, physical, mental, moral, and social have been the result. We ignored our untaught and helpless children, and great natural laws have worked out the penalty exactly proportional to the magnitude of the crime. Repentant, we are furnishing—too late, alas! for millions—the means of education, and are beneficently compelling their use.

Doubtless, too, compulsory labour is good for inmates of gaols. Despite the odium of the name under which the training is given, some few lads have by it been enabled the better to job along in life. Equally doubtless is it that the lack of compulsory labour is a bad thing for youth outside the gaol. Evils, physical, mental, moral, and social are the result. We are ignoring our unoccupied and helpless children, and great natural laws are working out the penalty exactly proportional to the magnitude of the crime. Repentant, we shall one day furnish the means of labour, and beneficently compel their use. And is it creditable to English love of fair play that things are as they are? Surely some day it will be considered worth while to be even-handed towards the gaoled and the ungaoled, not alone in provision for the idle brain, but also in provision for the idle hand. Why should everything provided by the State for the unemployed poor boy be across some bridge of crime? The State helps the young lieutenant, and does not make help conditional on his being turned out of a music-hall. The State helps the young artist, and does not make its help conditional on his being taken up on a charge of being drunk and disorderly. Why should the State's help to the young labourer be conditional on his picking a pocket?

Industrial Schools (so called) do not meet the case before us. They are to Reformatories not unlike what Houses of Correction are to government prisons. Like all State provisions for the luckless young, Industrial Schools require in candidates criminality of some sort somewhere to entitle to their benefits.

The Industrial Schools Act provides for children who are—

Runaways.

Progeny of convicts.

Precocious law-breakers.

Cronies of convicted thieves.

Victims of brutal parental cruelty.

Orphans, too idle to sell fish or matches.

For indeed one of a thousand who need the interposition of a compulsory labour law; and indeed for the special class needing the provisions of such an Act, it would seem to have been most unfortunately constructed. One half the children whom the School Board has taken up, who ought to be, were hoped to be, and supposed to be under its provisions, it has had to put down again. But this by the way.

Industrial schools provide for the child of an undoubted scamp, or for an undoubtedly scampish child. The act is one with all English legislation on affairs of the poor. It helps at the wrong end. It "quacks" with symptoms, and ignores diseases. It salves the rash, but leaves the vital cause alone.

But, what if these idle thousands are turned into workers?—have we not already a plethora of workers? What shall we do with them? Fairly consider what you are already doing with them. Would they not be better abroad than at home?—colonies of free men than colonies of paupers and convicts? If trained, they emigrate to the uninhabited States, what would England lose? Look at this difficulty in the broadest, highest interests! The welfare of a nation is not superior to great moral laws. Consider the question in the clear, warm light of manhood,—of manhood as a part of " the federation of the world," and you will fall in with the finely adjusted laws of personal and national prosperity.

CHAPTER III.

ORPHAN GIRLS IN "PLACE," PRIVATE AND PUBLIC.

YOUNG children are being constantly thrown on our London streets, their parents dead or dying. What becomes of these friendless thousands? A large proportion are girls.

Sometimes it is imagined that the motherless girl is absorbed by the demand for domestic servants. Domestic servants! What can she know of domestic service, trained, as she has been, in a home where tea was the one meal; the house, one dingy room; the routine of life, for her at least, nothing to do—save, perhaps, the lively duty of lugging about a child! The duties of "place" by her are utterly unknown. The customs of domestic life are mysteries, which she never knew—never cared to know. Imagine such a girl entering her teens and domestic service—an *orphan* girl with no home—all she has to offer, brute labour and cheap; and how can you be surprised to find the three following Penitentiary facts? First, out of 551 inmates, 423 had been servants; secondly, 303 had found refuge in their wretched life before the age of sixteen; thirdly, 387 were orphans!

Some light may be shed on a grave question by the following:

* * * * * *

On the steps of a London hospital stood a girl of about seventeen. A pair of lustrous eyes looked out upon the street, wet and sloppy with an early fall of snow, into which she seemed reluctant to venture. Under her arm was a small parcel. First one way and then another seemed to be the selected direction. A tippeted policeman passed and the girl inquired, "Which is the way to ——?" The question closed a sad chapter in a young life and opened one sadder still.

What had become of the girl's father was not known. She was just the child in which the rough seaman took delight. He loved the responsive thrill, the strong convulsive arms, the gushing kisses, when, kneeling on his knee, he pressed her warm young breast to his warm old one. Around his fate their hung a mystery. Since the day his ship sailed, four years before, no tidings of it or of its crew had reached the office to which it belonged.

Three months after her father had last visited his home her mother died. After her mother's death she was handed over to the care of her only known relation, an aunt, who had "work and only two children of her own." One front room for washing, one back room for sleeping, was the home of this charitable relative. Her two children were an invalid boy of eighteen, subject to fits, and a good-for-nothing son of nineteen, who hung about the docks for chance labour. In the front room they usually ate, in the back room they all always slept. A laundress this aunt had been for eighteen years, but her washing days were nearly done. Disease, hard work, dire poverty, and constant fretting over her afflicted child were fast bringing the long and bitter story of her life to its end.

Eight months gone and the girl's aunt was dead. Now she was without home, without money, without employment, without friends! Her work had hitherto been to clean up, to put out clothes, to help to mangle, and to go errands. Soon as the grave closed over her aunt the girl sought employment. Although living in a back slum, and that, too, a slum among acres of slums, her aunt had been proud to say that she had never eaten what she had not earned. No union officer or district visitor had ever left a crumb at her door. Again and again had she risked starvation rather than take the bread of charity or be beholden to the law.

First the girl tried to get a home with the mangle woman, but without more success than to be "let in for a night or two." Next she amused the neighbouring charwomen and laundresses by offering her youthful service to them. Then she turned to the clothes-basket mender, a handy shoemaker who lived near, and to the oilman, with whom her aunt had dealt for candles and soap. At the oilman's she found a service in his dark, damp cellar, with hardships to which the hulks would scarcely find a parallel. From this place in a few months she ran away. Now she applied at a servant's registry office with a view to being nurse. But "no character" written in the column assigned in the entry book to "References" was fatal. At every visit to the office her inquiry as to success was answered by "without appointment." Passing out of the office on the tenth or twelfth day disheartened and desperate, she was accosted by such a "beautiful lady," as the girl subsequently described her, and "so kind."

After a strict examination as to her relations, and discovering in the girl's evident honesty no reason to suspect the truth of her repeated assertion that she had "not one single friend," this "beautiful lady" at once offered her a place.

"Walk with me, my dear," said the woman. "I have taken care of many friendless girls in my day, and will be a mother to you if I can." Thus the search for employment ended in the place of "junior waiter" in a coffee-house. The qualities of person which had rendered her a thing of joy to her sailor father, and had darkened with sad forebodings the heart of her mother when her eyes were closing for ever on the girl, rendered her more valuable to her new mistress than the highest "character," and furnished her with ampler wages and board than she could possibly have earned by vigorous scrubbing or skilful needle.

At her new home, comfortable sofas, pleasant

smiles, and many youthful companions awaited her. At first she was half-servant, half-companion to the inmates. There was much life, little work, and good food and clothing. Many visitors attended the house in the evening and at intervals during the day. Here she mixed with girls who had lost their purity, but who had found a home. The majority of them were, like herself, young, orphan, and friendless. Their conversation with the "newcome" was chiefly of the privations of the over-squeamish girls who had been there but had left, of their subsequent sufferings, starvation, or suicide, of cases that had returned after having had "the nonsense" knocked out of them, but which could not find re-admission, "for madam never takes any back again, as she says, the chance once gone is gone for ever."

If the junior waiter entertained any idea of leaving her new home when she had become acquainted with its nature, it must have been dissipated by the force of all the associations and recollections of her bygone life. Her mother's bare garret, her hard-working aunt's dire poverty, the sexes and ages which had always shared her sleeping-room, her hardships in service at the oilman's, her many and fruitless efforts to obtain employment both before the oilman's place and after it, fully prepared her to believe the observation of her companion that "such a home was as good as their kind of girls can ever expect, and a great deal better."

* * * * * *

Smitten with fever, she had been conveyed from her place at the coffee-house to the hospital from the steps of which she inquired the way to ——. At the hospital new thoughts were inspired. There had occurred her first contact with high womanly purity and Christian teaching. To professional attention her nurse added a mother's tender interest and a Saviour's wise counsels. At parting they prayed together and wept together. The small bundle in the hand of the girl contained what the nurse had from her own stock given to her to "start again." With a few clothes, a little money, a pocket Bible, a book of hymns for revivals, and hope and faith in God, the orphan made her second venture on the world. But hope and faith were soon sorely tried.

First she thought of applying for "service," but to give references to the oilman would be vain, and to the lady at the coffee-house fatal. Recollecting the doom of "no character" in the registry-book, she abandoned this. She next turned to the City, and to the thousands fiercely struggling for employment she added one. Work proved scarce and hands too plentiful. Long had the little bundle of clothes given by the kind nurse been exchanged for a smaller bundle of pawn-tickets, and yet only just enough occasional work to keep up doomed hope. Then day by day, in boots which disclosed almost the whole stockingless foot within, in a gown too thin for summer wear, almost her only covering, to the City she tramped through snow and mud. Night by night she sat in her room in wet clothes by a fireless grate.

At the instance of the hospital friend she had taken a room for herself. It was only an empty attic, but when she first entered it she felt as Jacob on his Syrian common after his vision of the ladder and the angels. It was her Bethel. There, as the patriarch, she "vowed a vow, saying, If God will be with me, and will keep me in this way that I go, and will give me bread to eat and raiment to put on, then shall the Lord be my God." But heroic effort and long patience left her, in bitter winter, without "bread to eat" and without "raiment to put on."

One night she entered this room, and throwing herself starved and weary upon her bed, looking towards the little Bible on the window sill, as though it were its giver, madly she cried, "It's no use, it's no use, I'm not the sort for God," and covering her face with her thin black shawl, she sobbed and shrieked in blank despair. Day by day she had sought work for her fingers, and day by day, through wanton eyes and wanton tongues of warehousemen and clerks, she had learnt that she could make a market of her beauty. The one she had strenuously sought, the other she had heroically refused. But what must be the end?

Her early talks with her companions at the coffee-house came back to her recollections. So far as starvation and suicide were concerned, neither seemed unlikely to her. Was it not so, that "all in all, the life there was as good as friendless girls of their kind ought to expect?" What had been the experience of her honest, almost martyr's efforts after a virtuous and independent life?

* * * * * *

Two years gone, a crowd became acquainted with the hysterical laugh, the wild, reckless despair of a miserable woman in the custody of the police in a well-known thoroughfare. But they had not seen the struggles and tears which in solitude had often knitted the now brazen brow, and dimmed the now fiendish eye. They had not heard the vows and prayers which had arisen in an agony from the lips that now belched forth curses. At what cost the purer life had been exchanged for this, God only knew.

Countless lives may find in this a type.

On the class to which the child belonged law has bestowed its care. It has appropriated to itself the right to deal with the homeless under the Act for Industrial Schools, and hundreds of orphans find through its provisions food and training and home. Under that Act a companion of thieves may be apprehended and committed to the School. Had our orphan been on her way to theft, she might have found her way to one of these State-supported shelters. What could have possessed the framers of the Act to leave out altogether a clause which should have defined the notorious "companionship" to which a homeless girl is most likely to gravitate, it is impossible to say, but so it is. To the sons of the dead falls a happier lot than to the daughters of the dead.

Here are particulars. The number of inmates at a given day in the Industrial Homes of England were two thousand four hundred and sixty-five, of which eighteen hundred and twenty seven were returned orphans or homeless. Of the number which the State sent of these the proportion was as two girls to thirteen boys! The numbers in the schools of London alone being two hundred girls, thirteen hundred boys!

Could the wretched girl-orphan-lives, still in their teens, who are the wrecks of a neglectful law, turn at one time into the Palace Yard, what a horrid plea would they present for reform! Yet the plea might be in vain; for some makers of our law loudly uphold as the want of the nation a certain flourishing business in which it would appear young orphan girls do as a matter of fact play a major part.

The SOLDIER speaks of a great military, therefore national, demand. He protests against all influence which goes beyond regulating wisely the soundness of the supply. That economy, he says, is bad which does not deal with the affair as with ordinary food.

The PURE POLITICIAN—(the adjective is relative to the alleged principle on which the speaker considers the question, not to his moral character)—defends the omission in the Act of a clause which would cover that special companionship in a girl, which corresponds with thief-companionship in a boy, on the ground that the concomitant of the boy's companionship is an overt act against the State; the concomitant of the girl's is not such an act,—some would add, but precisely the reverse. To take theft even in its inceptive stage is therefore politically right, whilst to take the other thing at any time would be simply a violation of personal liberty.

MEDICINE and LITERATURE speak out on

this orphan's case. One reminds you of the rising race, "physical exigencies," and, warning in his voice, points to homes and contrasts the smallness of her disaster with the magnitude of alternative and worse evils! The other studies the morals of Europe, and waxes eloquent on her Exalted, her sacerdotal ministry! High Priestess of the universe! Smitten for the sins of the people!

But all this time the girl stands where in a certain book it is said this-kind-of-girl-"monger" will stand when the lights are lighted and the door is shut in another world,—out in the cold, and the boy is snugged in a home. We might pity the victim, and hope to make good the oversight, but for these startling Military, Political, Physiological, and Literary aspects of the theme.

Industrial-schools law is only one aspect of a many-sided and dismal affair. On the whole question of the "physical exigencies of the race," to borrow vague jargon with a certain obscure dignity about it and sufficiently plain for the purpose, legal justice is never so called because of its fairness. The boy snug, and the girl in the cold, is the monograph of British law,—one of the many kindred mysteries of the doings of a House which always opens its debates with prayer!

Were the House to amend the Industrial Schools Act so as to meet the case of girls under eighteen who had inherited a mother's instincts, but had lost a mother's care, what change might come over their present destiny! Meanwhile, waning strength, nearing nakedness, broken spirits, spent money, slack trade, and the "physical exigencies" of the race are doing their work.

PART III.—POVERTY.

CHAPTER I.

THE WORKHOUSE IN BRAINS OF RICH AND POOR.

WALLED up with Blue Books, crammed with statistics, full of theories, confident in plans, flattered by officials, ample in resources, we address ourselves to the well-being of the English poor.

Outlined in the vaguest forms are the subjects of our kingdom. Little know we, and less care we to know, the many fastidious social and moral distinctions which mark poor from poor. In our opinion, to the genus poor there are no species. Distance-haze hides away the personalities of the unhappy governed from the happy governor. Innocent of all differences, regardless of all individualities, recklessly insensible to all refinements—for what business have the dependent poor with differences, individualities, and refinements,—our only duty is to maintain the starving, our chief means to livery them in a common livery, feed them at a common table, house them under a common roof.

All unconsciously we are robbing, wounding, starving, driving across the sea the noblest blood in our hapless empire. We read reports and make laws, but of the effects of our laws we know nothing, save that everybody who has authority to speak says they are creating and fostering the very evils we intended them to destroy.

Would it not be the sound and only really English policy to introduce the representative element into the government of the poor?

What more stolidly stupid affair can be imagined than that of men trying to construct laws for the management of a far-removed people from the facts of official reports? Imagine one who had never walked a hospital trying to frame laws for times of epidemic from one of the chief physician's annual list of cases treated, or one who had never seen a ship trying to construct laws for difficult navigation from one of Lloyd's tables of wrecks, or one who had never spent a day in business trying to frame laws for the panics on 'Change! Where then is the reason for expecting that you are able to frame laws for the varied and complex exigencies of labour from knowledge furnished by the statistical and homilitical reports of your inspectors? To diminish the evils, soften the hardships, or achieve the possible good of poverty, are not exact knowledge and submissive obedience first conditions? Are there not great natural and artificial laws ruling in human beings under the exceptional conditions of poverty, cogent, well-defined, discoverable by those rulers who long to find them, and inflicting penalties on the ignorant disobedience of those who don't?

I will introduce the reader to one of his unenfranchised subjects, who at least deserves to have his say.

The scene:—a dingy panelled room, entered by a lockless, latchless door, fastened by a stick, as substitute for a padlock, in a staple and holdfast within. Furniture:—a chair, with the rushes which once formed the bottom hanging under the seat, now constructed of a narrow piece of unplaned timber tied across the frame with string; an empty soap-box turned on end, with a lighted candle in a candlestick, a teacup, and a pocket-knife on its top, giving the appearance of a table; a fire-place, furnished with a fender, a poker and kindling sticks, on one hob a brown earthenware teapot, on the other a little black kettle; a bed on the floor in the corner on one side of the fire, on the opposite side an open cupboard containing a cut loaf, a canister, and a little coal; and on the wall a small German quick-ticking clock. The hour: just gone four in the morning.

The hero:—a little dingy old man, unwashed, unshaven, shaggy-browed, of slouching gait, and blunt manner. His clothes, a dingy linen blouse, much the worse for wear, fustian trousers, well preserved in dirt, laced shoes never blacked, and a nebless cap. He has just swept up, lighted the fire, and is preparing a cup of tea—not, however, for himself. At half-past four, by a strap over his shoulder, he slings a moderate-sized hamper. The candle is out, the old man gone.

The public will become acquainted with our hero in the person of a dreamy-looking hawker, passing slowly through the middle-class streets of a London borough in the afternoon, crying, or rather saying in a low, melancholy, husky voice, "Cre-she! cre-she!"

Why notice the scene? the room is just like

countless rooms in which our social dregs find their resting-place. Why write of such a hero? such men are to be found by tens of thousands in every large town and city of the land. It is my object to lead you to hope that so it is, and in the light of his thoughts to judge your poor law.

Why write of him ?

Because citizens, philanthropists, Christians hardly yet understand that "things are not what they seem." Few persons looking upon this unpromising material would suppose that by intimate acquaintance he would be made to undergo a glorious transformation, the slouching gait be almost changed into the erect carriage of a proud and independent life.

Fourteen years he worked on roads, mending, scraping, watering. By an accident six ribs and his collar-bone were broken. A hospital repaired them. Then he began the work by which for twenty-five years he and his have been able to get along. With his wife he followed four children to their graves, then he buried her, and since, three more children. The only surviving member of his family is a girl of some eighteen years of age. She is in a decline—now a constant prisoner to the room, a frequent prisoner in the bed. It was for her that cup of tea was made.

"Her mother died on her," said the old man, in a subdued tone, as he nodded towards the bed where she lay, in the dark of the evening of a second interview; and then, after looking silently into the fire-grate for some time, he added, as though to himself, "She's her complaint, poor thing;" and in a few seconds in a still lower tone, "It'll be a dark shop about her."

Towards this girl, this dingy slouching old man cherishes, though an undemonstrative, yet no vague inoperative affection. To get her some tea, and "now and then a 'erring," and lay by from his earnings enough to put her away in her own coffin, when the necessity should come, is his present *raison d'être.*

Every morning he rises at four, and before half-past is trudging to a city market, some miles away; there he lays out a couple of shillings in cress, then trudges home again. "He might ride a bit," said his daughter; "it's along o' me as he won't." At about half-past eight he takes his first meal, ties up his purchase in bundles, and by noon is abroad again, trudging some three or four miles vending his stock. By four o'clock he is again in his room, with from a shilling to one shilling and ninepence as the varying profit of his trade. Thus he finds bread and roof for himself and his child. His habit is to lay by a few pence per day, accumulating in his banker's hands a fluctuating sum—fluctuating with the exigencies of sickness and funerals,—a sum now over four pounds.

The old man has three articles of a somewhat negative faith. Convinced of the evil of Beershops, City Missionaries, and "the Parish," he has formed a fixed determination to have no manner of dealings with these respective institutions.

The Beerhouse—indeed, beer he totally abjures, not because of its disasters to the health, and means, and chance of every second man, woman, and child of his acquaintance, but because horror of the workhouse is the cardinal point of his creed. He denies himself beer precisely as he denies himself flesh-meat, or the convenience of the cheap "workman's train" in the early morning. His major premis this—he won't go to the parish. His minor premis this—there's no way of using either meat, trains, or beer, and keeping off.

City missionaries are to him personages, possessed somehow of powers of relief. "A sister o' mine as was took bad was converted, as they calls it, at one o' ther meetin's. . . . . It's all along o' th' coals as they gets, for them as goes to ther meetin's," said he; and then, lowering his voice, and in a tone of half-amazement, half-disgust, "Sheff at th' shop says as she's been in th' report," a fact which to the speaker seemed the last proof of degradation, for he added, "none o' my blood's a been there afore. . . . . . . I'd as soon go to th' parish for my coal."

Little knowledge had our friend of Christian doctrines. Of the incarnation and death of our Lord he seemed as ignorant as though these sublime events had never transpired. The uses of vicars and ministers were to him learned mysteries. The only Christian agency he had ever seen at his door, which, but to fetch and to sell his cress, he seldom left, were officers, as he expressed it, to make "cants as gets coals;" and against their evil art he felt still strong enough, even in his shattered sixtieth year, to preserve his independence. In his opinion, city missionaries were welcomed by "paupers," and were sent away by everybody else.

Religion, however, he was not without. When, on first finding his daughter could not relieve her long hours of loneliness by reading, it was asked if the city missionary ever called to read with her? She replied, "No, sir, father won't have 'im." This led to the enquiry, "Does your father not like religion?"—not that the enquirer thought the two things necessarily identical. "O, yes," was her reply, "when he *sees* it. Mother was a good woman, he says, and he's fond o' bits o' texts and little hymns as she was fond of. He taught me 'em, and now I says 'em to 'im, he forgets."

The apparatus of his undemonstrative religion was probably invisible. The creed of his religion contained possibly but one word, and that one word was "God." God had taken his wife. God, too, was building heaven; but what God was, or what heaven was, he never conceived. To him God's only incarnation was in his dead wife. The Light of the world gleamed into his heart, if at all, reflected by her. It was she, too, that abolished death. Dying was, if anything, going to her. He seemed to associate the idea of God only with the memory of his wife. Possibly, heaven was also outlined to his imagination in the shadowy form of his wife. His favourite text was her favourite, "The Lord is my Shepherd," and following verses. His favourite hymn was hers, 'There is a house not made with hands." Why these things were so, was he obliged to know before his unintelligent experience could become religion?

Whether he had a heaven or not, he had, undoubtedly, a perdition, and that perdition was "the parish!"

Vague might be his ideas on other points, vivid enough were they here! Reciting his thoughts, he became a heated youth again—"The parish! The parish!" said the old man, concluding an excited and possibly somewhat extravagant harangue—"the p-a-r-i-s-h! and leave her!" Then, in deeper feeling but exhausted voice, bringing down his uplifted hand to his knees, and looking through a tear into the fire—"God help these old legs o' mine!"

Seven children and one wife he had followed to the grave, and the relief of his sorrow he found in the fact that none had he followed but in "their own coffin," and the prize of life to our old friend is expressed in this strange happiness—to sleep at last in his own coffin. Not to die, to use his own expression, "like a scamp on the parish:" to struggle on in his daily rounds, to keep body and soul honestly together, to pay rent, and the doctor, which in his vocabulary meant a neighbouring chemist, and then to close his daughter's eyes, and at last to close his own eyes, assured that there is still in the hands of his banker, the old iron dealer down the street, sufficient to pay for the shadow and shelter of a freeman's grave—this is the ambition of the down-looking, slouching old man.

* * * * * *

In the city crowd and bustle how often may the reader pass, beneath a rude exterior, ideals of independence, the existence of which, least of all the strength and majesty of which, he has but little suspicion. The fawning manner or slouching gait of a worn-out street hawker may be its garb. Undoubtedly much of the animal enshrined our friend. Much even of the lowest and most unimpressible class, but animals are not capable of this kind of life. A devotee of independence, to it he offered the sacrifice of his creed, translated into the acts of a daily, an hourly heroism. How many would be found to be like him, if their fellow-citizens but knew them better?

This possibility is no matter of indifference to the Christian. May not the masses be more Christian than theology has dared to conceive? Could we lift the veil that hides the true, because the deepest, life of man, how many from uncivilised street and barbarous room—but queer specimens of humanity—would come to be counted in God's host, heroically struggling through daily duty, temptation, and sacrifice, to a glorious rest.

Given among our city masses such a character as was hidden in our unpromising friend; and surely there is in city masses rudimental greatness—greatness awaiting nobler Christian workmen, finer, more perceptive Christian sympathy to call it into life; greatness showing itself even in grim and comical ways, yet capable of a patience, a perseverance, and a suffering, which it would be the glory, as it ought to be the ambition, of the Church to cultivate.

But this is digression. What is the meaning of this starving honour? This pinching? This dying, rather than touch "the parish?"

In a search for the reason, a little imagination will stand you better than blue books. Look through the eyes of a man, whose conception of a workhouse is derived from experience in a low part of London, who sees what it has actually achieved in his own street. I will particularise, so far as might be chiefly seen from our hero's window; and as taken down carefully from his own lip.

Next door is a widow who has her loaves taken off her because she "spoke sharp" to the officer—on whose good word all depends—about what he did to a neighbour. In a house on the opposite side, upstairs, there's a loving old couple who have jogged on together for forty years; they have with them a dead daughter's child of ten, because they won't break up their "home," and give up the girl-company and care; how can they? they get no relief; the old man has bronchitis. Downstairs was an idle disreputable couple, but too glad to be split; they have gone into the "house." Next door to these was a sick man, and his wife and family. Because, when well, he was provident and enrolled in a sick-club, from which he obtained four shillings a week, he could not obtain so much as a loaf. A little lower was a woman, who being unmarried had been treated "like a lady" in four successive confinements—the historian adding in parenthesis, "an' they say as there's ninety o' that sort in a year." On the floor above her, there had been a "bad" woman who became insane; she found its lodgings. On the floor above her, a widow who for sending her boy to "a job got some relief knocked off," whilst, as he said, "women as don't look after their lads had it kep' on." A widow that he knew in another street had gone into the "House," as they wouldn't help her out, "An' then when she'd give up her two chil'der, 'as they made her do, they boarded 'em out with the sexton's widow, two or three doors down t' same street." Another family whom he knew, "they made go in, an' they came out without a roof an' without a penny." From the very room in which he is now living, there went the filthiest debauchee in the district, who, by his profligacy, brought on diseases which totally unfitted him for work.

Weigh well the workhouse as it exists, not in the brains and folios of a Local Government Board, but as it exists in city, town, and village, especially as it haunts the brain of rude but honest observers; and how can you wonder if it should be regarded possibly as a seat of tyranny, and certainly as the drainage of vagabondism, little and big!

Surely to Guardians, Relieving Officers, Masters, and all persons familiar with board-room revelations, the objection of an any-way fastidious mind to a workhouse is no mystery. Yet remember, gentlemen, darkness wraps away from even your practised eye the real characters for whom you provide a home. Imagine the position of one who has known twenty years of the history of a man who, when on his guard, in five minutes let out of his real life enough to sicken and horrify you! Why he should shun the house of such men, can it be difficult for you to conceive?

It is all very well for people who are not likely to have to go to the workhouse, to consider it from a purely abstract point of view; in Acts of Elizabeth, and articles in a Quarterly, or speeches of eloquent M.P.'s. But that was not our hero's way. He began with the workhouse as he began with everything else, from the point of consciousness. Facts had been his educator. Your learned discussions he had not heard, your actual works he had been obliged to see, and of the merits of these he knew far better than you. Hunger had often pinched him, but then the idea of your "House" had always pinched him more! What fellowship has he with incorrigibly idle, dissipated, dishonest, and suspicious neighbours you compel to come in, and the occasional tramps,—to London workhouses admitted at the rate of three hundred and eighty thousand a year,—which you have added to them? No surprise to him would be the revelations of your House discipline-book; nor would he be at all startled to find, your handcuffs, strait-jackets, and cells notwithstanding, that in ten years you had to call in the police to your aid above sixteen thousand times.

Herschels know something of the sun, but

surely the inhabitants, if there be any, know more, tabulated spectroscopic revelations notwithstanding. The apparatus of the Blue Book may be, and doubtless is, a very fine and ingenious affair; but, after all, may not the inhabitant of the poor man's world have something to say which you don't know, and would do well to hear? Why should you not admit somehow such men as our hero—women, too,—into your councils?

Little knows the poor fellow of grammar; his reasoning, too, is a rough blundering affair; but he has brought up a family through all the vicissitudes of labour and sickness under many years of your government. He can tell you how honest men came to need your care; how when they came to need it, they looked at your terms, they shook their heads, they died; how less noble spirits closed with your terms and lived. Don't laugh at him, his neighbour was a martyr, his sister too! He is serious—he may be one himself.

To your exalted vision, the inhabitants of one street are all upon a level. Amongst themselves there are ranks and grades, tramps and peers, plains and very Matterhorns of rugged nobility. You ignore this, hence all your maladministration.

I remember a rough but most worthy woman to whom the House relief had been offered, saying in justification of her not accepting it, "I never knew anybody go into the House as I should like to foller, but a cripple lad as is dead, he *was* a nice feller. Believe me, sir, most o' them as 'as gone from our street would shame t' bad place itself. While I can stand over a tub," said she, drawing herself into a rigid and quivering erectness, "I'll never mix with such a lot." The woman had four children to inherit her spirit. She did not stand over her tub much longer. The chances of long life are only secured to baser folks. Little cared she for spacious rooms, ample food, neat frocks, and clean, starched bonnets. To her, unclean birds were unclean birds, a fine cage notwithstanding. Had you visited "the House," you would have seen only clean clothes and clean faces; but beneath the clothes behind the faces, she must have seen hearts, histories!

When Faraday would not take a state pension until Lord Melbourne had apologized for the insulting conditions under which it was offered, he inherited the pride of a certain poor woman, who possibly—in her room over the mews in Newington Butts—had known what it was to be at her wits'-end for bread. Given her necessities, and the State provision would have been only open on terms as haughty and unbearable to the humble, straitened woman, as, in the day of his honour, State provision was open to her illustrious son. All sons are not Faradays. But in how many thousands of widows, sempstresses, and charwomen is the spirit of Mrs. Faraday, of the room on the mews in Newington Butts! Amongst such, the present bent of your laws—not so intentioned, no doubt—is to crush all that you ought to foster.

And so, under the dictation of laws, men and women, in their straitened hours, are finding their place — the more honourable, their place, the less honourable, their place; and it is neither to the credit nor to the advantage of the land that these places are what they are. The misfortune to the country and hardship to the poor is, that the more humane and independent is hunger, the more the chance that starvation will win the day, and its victims be cut off from the land of the living, or doomed to emaciated life.

The humane and independent poor, it is said, are few. Be it so. Is it likely the numbers will be increased under the present system of poor-law selection? By the disabilities under which you place them in their inevitable hours of weakness, are they helped in their struggle for existence?

And on the other hand, if all physical disadvantages are to be removed from the surroundings of those who are willing to enter the "Union"—if you provide the scientifically correct number of cubic feet of breathing space for each, serve to them varied, wholesome and ample food, force upon them regular and suitable habits, watch with vigilance their symptoms, and nurse with care their ailments, who can doubt that the full-fledged pauper will become, physically at least, the healthiest, sturdiest specimen of the race, and against all comers — children of shopkeepers and parish curates—win the corporeal prize.

Visions of a day when the House shall extinguish the pauper race it is said haunt powerful minds. By its test independence is to be fostered and a great work is to be done in raising the hungry world. How little must such minds heed the facts of experience, observation and science, to dream such dreams. Hardly is it true that paupers as well as foes are killed with kindness. Surely the present system of pauper provision stands self-condemned. Is it not by its very perfectness a paradise of fools? With degradation of soul it increases the chances of life.

Could the whole story be written, the story of the woes you have caused to the sequestered poor: of the ailments you have caused to children, the lives of fresh-made mothers you have sacrificed, the agonies and embarrassments you have brought upon fathers,—what a magnitude of deadly work would be disclosed! And this not by your niggardliness; you have been lavish enough; nor by your neglect, for you have been fussy and meddlesome enough; but by your oppression of pride, oppression through ignorance, red-tape-informed ignorance. How ample, too, would be the illustration of the Darwinian theory in the degree to which by poor-relieving agencies in city, town, village, and hamlet, you had been able almost to eliminate that human variety known as the prouder poor!

Romance has done bold things in depicting the victims of wrong; but were the deeds of Whitehall in the haunts of poverty faithfully depicted the most popular romances would lie unopened, at least by those who love to read in tears. And remember these *are* written to the Poor. Of all this complicated, bungling, suffering and slaughter, you have been the author; because you, who knew them not, and did not try to know them, would govern.

CHAPTER II.

THE POOR LAW NOT A LAW FOR THE POOR.

"THE best things for me," said an agent of United States' lands, "are slack times and your Poor Law; the net's all cod then."

Without challenging the correctness of his piscatorial figure—"It's not our Poor Law," was the Englishman's reply, "we have no Poor Law. The thing which goes by that name is a law for such of the poor as are not English."

Was the reply correct? Has the country ever yet directly and simply faced the problem of the poor? Generations ago it devised ways and means for the extermination of supposed vagabonds. Mended, amended, and remended, it has applied these to the suppression of paupers, both of which ways and means have unfortunately and somewhat comically turned out to be ways and means for the maintaining and propagating of both vagabonds and paupers ; but through as many generations, have not the *bonâ-fide* poor been left to take care of themselves ?

Was it indeed this fact which, occurring to the Poor Law Board, led them conscientiously to drop their old name, and to adopt one which should be more consistent with the semi-penal character of their administration ? The "Local Government Board" does surely better befit their doubtless necessary department of criminal law. If the reason of this change of name be as the facts of the case would lead one to suppose, to no passage will the moralist of the future point with prouder confidence in illustration of the power and nature of honesty, than to that passage in English history which records this act of the Poor Law Board. They changed their name because strictly speaking their law was not a law for the poor!

What wonder then if the misery and sufferings of the masses of the simply poor are almost unrelieved by the millions in which the British taxpayer is mulcted for the things which are called laws of the poor. How should means devised for one thing be expected to do another? If you imagined that you could meet all the necessities of government by laws framed for rogues, or all maladies possible to the body by antibunion salve,—what would you deserve for your pains! How much profounder the folly which deals with the life and death question of straitened humanity on precisely analogous principles!

If the poor were to be classified, they would be roughly divisible into three sections: An immense number who are victims of vice, whose poverty is permanent, who suffer chiefly in body and are much seen about; an immense number who are the helpless victims of providential fate, whose poverty is permanent, who suffer both in mind and in body, and are little seen about; a smaller number who are victims of a great variety of more or less temporary causes, whose poverty might be temporary were temporary means available, who for lack of such means are constantly recruiting the hopelessly poor, who also suffer in mind and body and are little seen about. The homes of the first and second sections, generally speaking, divide the poorest quarters of the city; the homes of the third section are *in transitu* intermixed with the homes of the better class workmen.

Surely it is the second and third great divisions which suffer most, need and deserve most help. But in your lavished millions for the poor, of the third class almost none share; of the second, only the less English half; and of the first, almost the whole. You put your hands deeply into your pockets in a ratio exactly the reverse of the suffering, the deserts, and the possibility of aiding the man who takes your money.

Where is the wonder? Your only State organization for the poor assumes poverty bad in the lump, and enacts accordingly. On the same level it meets all the hungry, be they sturdy vagabonds, sly scamps, or honest men and women. It requires all to submit to the same "test," apply at the same "Board," work in the same "yard," scramble for bread at the same depôt, and to stand rank and file in the same street, before the same staring public, to receive their sixpences at the same office window! If I am a crafty scamp or a knavish profligate, these requirements wont make me a bit more reluctant to share in your provision, but the moment I cease to be either, difficulties begin and continue to increase in every stage as I rise in moral grade.

But more, your provision may require "complete and entire separation" of husband and wife, parent and child. Ignoring all other distinctions, you divide your house into the great general departments of Male,

Female, Children. Your creed runs thus:—First, families who come to you are the "worst enemies" of each other; 2ndly, it is cheaper to maintain them in your house, in herds, than out of doors on the family basis—cheaper, because you know that, to thousands of the poor, your policy is a home-breaking, heart-breaking affair, than submit to which it is easier to them to starve and die. You have the heart to argue thus; at all events, in your official circular to the distributors of your rate-raised millions you do argue thus:—Out of every ten English poor families it is probable that under the HOUSE "TEST" only one will be un-English enough to succumb and accept your condition, therefore it follows that by applying that test the cost of helping the families of nine out of ten may be saved. (*Vide* First Report of Local Government Board, 1871–2, pp. 66.)

You apply a test which, if love and honour survive the wreck of fortune, must be economical,—to which with ease and dignity brain-demoralized, heart-degraded parents alone will submit, and call that your poor law!

But it is argued, "We've saved the Rates!"

Has it not occurred to you Poor Law Economists that the sum spent in helping the family of the ones in tens might still more be diminished if bread were retained until the famine-stricken applicant were willing to go to gaol! Surely a starving man could not object. Before the issue of your next circular, would it not be well for you to learn your lesson more perfectly, to consider with the prime author of your policy, "What will a man give in exchange for his life?"—whether, by wringing more from human suffering, you might not further still reduce the chances of its closing with your terms, and from the fiend-lip from which that query first dropped win more deserved and ample praise.

Meanwhile, a grave question is needing

answer. Have you saved the rates?—have you not rather mortgaged them, and on most disastrous terms? Go down to the homes of the finer-spirited poor, see in the home-loving labourer, in his furniture, clothes, tools, and his own and family's muscles dwindling away the effect of your test, and answer, can this finally even save the rates?

How comes this dark anomaly in English law? The reply is that England fancies she has a Poor Law, and, amid the bustle and confusion of her railway making, telegraph buying, University reforming, Church disendowing, Army organizing, Alabama settling, Ballot enacting, Suffrage extending, has not time to look the fact in the face that no such thing exists. Your present organization was constructed to face noxious idleness. Your law was made to repress the incorrigible vagrants, your house to roof moral rubbish, your rate to maintain a semi-gaol. Doubtless the system is mended, patched, let out, taken in, but it still remains a system for human nuisances. Under its operation you take away civil, connubial, parental rights,—set aside the man's country's and his nature's laws. You raise your workhouse roof, whitewash, warm, and ventilate on the most approved principles; but what cares the honest husband for your reform whilst you assume the functions of Death, and cancel his marriage vow?—or what avails it all to the widow whose widowhood you bereave of her children!

England has no Poor Law! She has an elastic, vagabond law, which some do-the-best-we-can sort of guardians humanely stretch, sometimes tear, so as best they may to cover the necessities of the poor not vagabonds. But this they do in a manner which to the visiting, law-loving official is altogether shocking.

Candidly, all class feelings apart, what is your policy to the victims of poverty? What else than veritable red-raggism? In what does its principle differ from the principle of the stupidest, harshest, most horrible procedure of the French Revolution? It is the strong arm of the leveller in the kingdom of poverty. You would bring down the *noblesse* of the state you rule, dismantle their *châteaux*, degrade their rank, rob their constitutional rights, defraud husband of wife and wife of husband, exchange freedom's dress for the badge of a serf, and lodge them with the scum of their social and moral world. What is it but, under the name of a Poor Law, a legalized attack on the foundations of workmen's society?—a blind or reckless insensibility in the class which is up to the feelings and rights of the class which is down?

Maybe you deride the idea of the foundations of workmen's society,—a poor labourer's *château* and distinctions of labourer's rank. Be it so; rough fustian is able to show and ever will show a mettle you never dreamed of in your vulgar respectability. There may be much of the animal about the hungry fellow, but his love, his pride, and his liberty he'll hold against the world.

Whoever has passed wide awake through a work-famine well knows that whilst the despicable feed, the manful starve, chafe, perchance cross the sea.

"Where is C.?" said a large employer to his foreman when good times had come back again.

"He's at ——, in the State of ——."

"I'd give a lot for him just now. That's a tickle job as John's at; he's not half the man for it."

"Well, C.'s got a few acres fenced in, and a shanty and a cow or two, and he's doing well."

"Hang it, that's the way with pluck!" was the reply. "Bad times plays the deuce with us!"

John had fed on the parish—much against his will, by the way—but C. had said he'd die first, and being a through and through good fellow, when he had used up his savings was able to borrow enough to take his sore-stricken soul to another land.

Given a panic, and the emigrant ship becomes the 'May-flower' of Labour. Men who can neither stand your workhouse "test" nor your degrading out-door relief; men who married early —no sin surely—who cannot live on nothing, nor stand three months' divorce as the price of bread, who are "a cut above" huddling and scuffling for loaves and sixpences, though their coats are nothing to be proud of; rough, sturdy-bodied and rough, sturdy-hearted men crowd into America. By wounding conscience, English law founded America's foremost city; by wounding pride, English law is filling America's most prosperous States.

But the mettle which will not close with your terms apart, more disastrous still is the effect of your law on the famine-driven multitudes who will. One day, for very bread's sake, panic-stricken fathers submit; they consent to plead with the idle and jostle with the scamp, to take your livery and break up their home. Obedient to your bidding, they pocket their pride, and—fatal victory!—think you are they ever likely to take it out again? The event once accomplished, nothing can blot out from their history, and its effects nothing can take from their blood. Once cured, the pride-disease seldom returns. Again and again, the dociled spirit you find with bread, provide with doctor, aid in rent, and, having been asked at your "Board" whether he received anything from a club, having obtained help because, on his Maker's name, he could swear that he never received a farthing from a club in his life, your captive swears life-long fealty to the Union, and the once vanquished rebel against his country's laws for the poor goes his way and sins no more.

Whatever may or may not be the chemistry of workhouse bread, one thing is clear,—little paupers soon grow big upon it, and once a customer, a customer for ever.

Not to be calculated are the evils remotely as well as directly consequent on your raid on the manhood of the poor. Generation after generation the natural complications of poverty become more unnaturally complicated. By far the most terrible fact is that demoralized parents leave their substance to their children. Exorcised from the fountain, pride is not found in the stream. Imagine the mettle of a child whose whole ideal of life has been gained in a home in which being "a cut above" anybody you made positively illegal! How can you be astonished if he be bred up humble,—humble enough to go anywhere, to be anything, to get your loaf? In his limited experience you help such, and leave all the rest alone. How can you speak harshly of your own begotten child? Might not the negro as reasonably reprove his family for their frizzy heads! What have you left undone that you could have done and which you ought not to have done practically to teach your victim that anti-pride was, for his kind at least, the law of the land?

The so-called Poor Law system is one grand State organization for suppressing the manhood of the poor, and in labour-panic makes slaughter of its enemy on a scale of awful magnitude, thrusting its sword through the heart of the yet unborn.

CHAPTER III.

A NATIONAL CLUB.—£8,000,000 FOR THRIFT.

An appeal is sometimes made to the extent of pauperism for the purpose of showing that the "House test" must be yet more vigorously and impartially applied. Is it possible that any but men let out of Bedlam, or men who believe that Poor Government is superior to all natural law, can imagine the consequences of such a course to be other than evil? Diminished rates, perchance, but certainly diminished manhood! How can your screw reduce pauperism whilst it exterminates the best things in its victims? Men may die and rise again, but manhood, never!

Did it ever occur to you to query what might have been the condition of the motley group scrambling for bread at your relief depôts, had not your imperious will throttled their helpless father's pride? A barbarous fellow he might have been, but under other treatment he was capable of a better progeny than this. Could some modern Solomon devise expedient whereby the State might rush to throw her arms around her own proper child, how many of the 100,000 paupers would she embrace, and how many of the eight millions which they cost would prove to be the price of unintended parentage!

Was not our present rate mortgaged full twenty years ago? And what will our sons do but pay debts of our policy, as we pay debts of our fathers' policy? From our law-degraded, law-demoralized homes they will inherit a house-fed, blue-jacketed, gingham-frocked, pitiable progeny.

What if we try a new experiment! What if we try to preserve through distressful hours a father's pride, provide means whereby the rough fellow, with his young wife and little lads and lasses, might tide through his no-work months; obtain bread which should nourish spirit as well as flesh, breathe an atmosphere in which manhood and matter could live; means which should preserve to him his freedom, his freedom's name, his freedom's rights,—should we not help him a whole man through his trial, reduce the present evils of poverty to their minimum, and to the future send down children inheriting their father's spirit as well as their father's frame? Would not such a course, if possible, be as surely followed by good consequences as our present course is followed by consequences which are evil? Should we not economise—I will not say in gold, though that is certain—but in our country's cardinal glory?—and if the means cost twice eight millions, would not the picture of more manful men be cheap!

The vital question is, is such a thing possible?—can the means be devised? The means are devised. For units of British labour, the scheme is an accomplished and a successful fact. If what is possible to private Associations is, *mutatis mutandis*, possible to a whole community, the scheme only awaits our will. Let the principle of the mutual benefit be taken up by the community; let there be established a national "Club;" let it provide for the exigencies of labour, of sickness, of accidents, of age, and of death; let it be open to every man, woman, and child; let its payments be payments spread over a number of years or payments in the lump; let it be in no sense penal; let its benefits rank as a sick club allowance, a a fire insurance payment, a disabled soldier's pension, or an ex-minister's annuity; and let it by no means be a department of "Poor Law" administration. The demoralizing association would be fatal. Let it be a department of the Board of Trade, and why not? Let it rank among new institutions of the State, and be worked under new auspices—let its benefits be available as a right, a purchased, proprietary right—and the thing is done.

It would be profoundly foolish to imagine that this arrangement would abolish "the House." Let it remain; let sturdy vagabonds and noxious profligates in the hour of their famine be sent to it. Confiscate their liberty, divorce them, take their children from them, livery them, label them, and let the name pauper stick. But in the name of everything you honour, save the honester folk from the sense of humiliation—always strongest in the best—of being labelled with the same name, housed under the same roof, fed at the same table, regulated by the same semi-criminal get-up, go-out, come-in, go-to-bed rules, and scrambling at the same office for a loaf. Ought not the infliction of such indignity on helpless and guiltless poverty, to smite the nation's cheek with the fire of intolerable shame?

True Poor Legislation will begin when law takes the small scheme of a club, lifts the scheme to the rank of a State policy, removes from it all that is uncertain and hazardous, amplifies its objects, cheapens its payments, augments its advantages, and builds it large enough to embrace the million. Let this be done; let it be announced that State help is henceforth servant of honour, that the consequences of thrift shall be life-long freedom and domestic and civil rights, but of thrift only; and who can doubt that some of the darkest phases and most difficult problems of poverty would gradually pass away?

Might we not thus even attract the pauperised? What would be the probable influence of such legislative action on men constructing their ideas of life under the present system. Now, to tens of thousands thrift and hand-to-mouth living have almost identical ends. The House is but a question of a few weeks, and meanwhile hard struggling pride gets nothing, whilst lowly minds receive 4*s*. per week. But would the pauperisable think the same thoughts if for sixpence a-week he could secure bread *plus* liberty, but only thus? Would it not be worth while to see whether our millions devoted to the weal of thrift would accomplish results at all differing from the results of millions devoted to the weal of thriftlessness!

And who, professing to know anything of the history of private clubs, but will be sure of the wonderful influences of a club of the STATE, where the money paid would be invested in a certainty, where there would be no hazard, and the advantages and terms be better suited to the pinched masses? Given such superior conditions, and club members, now counted by tens, would speedily be counted by thousands, and by the ratepayers' wealth the masses would be tempted towards their own and their country's good.

In this direction is not something needed, ought not something to be done? Year by year commerce more complicated, competition more keen, the loom-war of nations more fierce; the humblest workers in the thickest of the conflict, under the hottest of the fire. Can that nation be wise—not to say, can it be just—which provides no ambulance of which the sufferers can avail themselves without dishonour and shame? Deserters from the great army of labour, court-martial if you will, but surely you agree that to the wounded in the struggle of existence should be decreed some better fate.

Countless thousands of poor are guiltless of their poverty. On the plains of Bethnal Green, as well as on the heights of Alma, men borne down are less fortunate, not always less brave. Do you not own that thousands cannot make daily bread, and thousands more, though they can make daily bread, cannot lay one farthing by; and that to multitudes of these the workhouse can afford no help, since they have a maybe rude but laudable pride?

Is it not your duty fairly to weigh the condition of a quarter of a million in London alone, whose unaided and normal condition is the verge of hunger and pennilessness; to imagine if you can the fearful consequences of even a week or two's no-work, and to ask whether their misery at such times is not the result of your culpable neglect?

Can it have failed to occur to you that panic, at least, must deserve some new and special provision? Do you not think that with the hammer pre-eminently the modern sword, the stake of our factories as national a stake as the stake of Waterloo, the prosperity of the Clyde a blockade of the Thames, the quarrels of presidents, a siege of Manchester,—schemes should be devised to insure that no wounded or veteran labourer shall either die or live like a dog?

What can possibly possess us to provide forts against the contingent fire of foreign guns, and yet provide no manner of safety against the actual raids of foreign ware—against possible blood-shedding, and not against actual blood-drying? Is not life attacked by starvation as English as life attacked by steel? and is not the duty of their legislative protection equal?

But why reason thus? Legislative provision for the poor is already made, but really made for one class of the poor, for that class for whom its terms are suited—the incorrigible and all others who have no objection to associate with them. Compare the claims of these persons upon State provision with the claims of the average disabled artisan, labourer, sempstress, and small shopkeeper, and with which rests the advantage? Can a single reason be urged in favour of provision for men and women who neither deserve nor value an honourable name, nor civil nor domestic rights, which does not become a reason, *à fortiori*, when urged in favour of provision for men and women to whom both honourable name and civil and domestic rights are identical with life? If in necessity it is made possible and easy to the one class to share in the treasure of the national purse, must there not be wrong-headedness somewhere which in like necessity makes it impossible to the other class to do the same, except on unreasonable and pain-forcing terms!

The results of our present policy are, happily, satisfactory to not a single subject of the Queen who knows anything about them. Local Government Board, Guardians, Workhouse masters, Ratepayers are in a hopefully grumbling condition, and even the thoroughbred pauper himself has in him enough of the traditional Englishman to hate his conqueror, —a lingering something makes a wily sinner of him. By a rough law of take and give, he eats your bread, accepts your shilling, and tricks you if he can.

Conclusion.

We are at the beginning of a parliament for children. Long has the children's turn waited, at last it has come. The movement which starts in education must extend over all their affairs.

The hour is great, and the greatness of the hour is equalled by the greatness of its difficulties. The undomesticated child is the real gravity of the case. To consider calmly, estimate justly, and devise wisely on his affairs, is the great debt of the past, the one hope of the future. On the public sentiment of the hour everything depends. Pray let us look at his case in the right mood, or leave it alone. Far better things as they are, than reformation based on error.

This volume is given to the public in the hope that, if it fail to win favour for its practical suggestions, it may not fail to produce a happier and kindlier feeling towards the great bulk of the big and little victims of dirt, disease, disaster, dissipation, and despair. Not as charity merely, but as bare justice such a feeling is inevitable, exactly in the measure in which we come to close and intimate knowledge. The facts — selected out of not a few similar occurrences within the writer's own observation—appeal for themselves to the good sense and candour of true English hearts.

The result of my efforts may, in some cases, be censure. I may be credited with ignoring moral distinctions, merging them in the depths of a weak sentimentalism and the like.

Be it so.

If, on the other hand, in a few instances there should be awakened a kindlier feeling towards the outcasts, the censure will be easy to bear, and the trifling labour amply rewarded.

Simply a kindly feeling! Is not that a weak thing? Yes, weak indeed. Often have I unflaggingly worked, heart to heart, shoulder to shoulder, with some wild, ignorant, yet still noble, disinterested, and aspiring lad, whose good in him had touched something in me, and roused it to impulses which felt like brotherhood, only to find a complication of opposing circumstances perfectly maddening and hopeless. Nevertheless, my faith in kindly feeling is not a whit feebler. Truly, it is one of the weak things; but is it not one of the weak things of God?

Who can tell what, by transient knitting of soul and soul, has been done for a lad and for his God! One step beyond confidence in man lies the new and higher faith in God. Mutual hope in effort, and dejection in failure may at least bring within one step of the threshold of immortality. Fruitlessly you seek to see one a smith, may you not still see him a saint? Success is not the doing what one would; it is doing what one can. God is king. God is on the side of the heart, therefore somehow, love is victory.

Especially in great cities, with the outcast, things have gone wrong—many things, things physical, social, and religious, long and fearfully wrong—and of late with ever-increasing speed.

A kindly feeling will patiently and hopefully unravel what appears to other moods the tangled and hopeless "mess" of our civilisation. It will be the free, spontaneous, and mighty cause of a new world.

Through the artisan it will work towards forbearance.

Through the landlord towards better dwellings.

Through statesmen towards wiser laws; and

Through the Church towards redeeming lives.

The grandest, most beautiful, most victorious things in history, a kind feeling has inspired.

The most touching scenes—the scenes which stand out in the world's one incomparable life, and live before the eye as the proudest achievements of the Son of God, are due to His kindly carriage towards the outcast. The abandoned swarmed around Him, drawn by the fresh and unspeakable charms of pity and care. When He met a fallen life, for whom nobody else yearned, it seemed as though he could forgive everything and forget everything save the sins of those their accusers. It was an agony to Him to see a sheep without a shepherd, an unhappy life without another life wiser and stronger to care for it, and His agony became anger when on such fell the blows of virtue instead of the tears of pity. In this He left an example.

The power of feeling has not changed, the

Spirit of the Nazarene is still the same. To the heart it gives emancipation, to the conscience victory. Still, it is to the outcast a fresh birth. What a spectacle to men and to angels would Jesus be in Wapping or Ratcliffe Highway! In a sublime agony the stones would cry out!

Meanwhile, the reader may wed some outcast youth to hope and fortune, or carry light and warmth into the eye, and brain, and heart of outcast age, and thus fate somebody to a happier and better life.

PRINTED BY
TAYLOR AND CO., LITTLE QUEEN STREET, LINCOLN'S INN FIELDS.

Titles in This Series

1

Jelinger C. Symons

Tactics for the Times: As Regards the Condition and Treatment of the Dangerous Classes

London, 1849

2

William Hepworth Dixon.

The London Prisons: With an Account of the More Distinguished Persons Who Have Been Confined in Them, To Which is Added, A Description of the Chief Provincial Prisons

London, 1850

3

C. B. Adderley

Transportation Not Necessary

London, 1851

with

Charles Pearson

What Is to Be Done with Our Criminals? A Letter to the Right Honorable the Lord Mayor

London, 1857

4

Rev. John T. Burt

Results of the System of Separate Confinement as Administered at the Pentonville Prison

London, 1852

5

Frederic Hill

Crime: Its Amount, Causes and Remedies

London, 1853

6

Rev. Joseph Kingsmill

Chapters on Prisons and Prisoners, and the Prevention of Crime

London, 1854

7

George Laval Chesterton

Revelations of Prison Life; with an Enquiry into Prison Discipline and Secondary Punishments

London, 1856. Two volumes.

8

Rev. Walter L. Clay

Our Convict System

London, 1862

with

Sir Joshua Jebb

Reports and Observations on the Discipline

& MANAGEMENT OF PRISONS
London, 1863

9
Rev. Benjamin Waugh
THE GAOL-CRADLE, WHO ROCKS IT?
London, 1873

10
Edward W. Cox
THE PRINCIPLES OF PUNISHMENT, AS APPLIED IN THE ADMINISTRATION OF THE CRIMINAL LAW, BY JUDGES AND MAGISTRATES
London, 1877

11
FIVE YEARS' PENAL SERVITUDE BY ONE WHO HAS ENDURED IT
London, 1884

12
John Campbell
THIRTY YEARS' EXPERIENCE OF A MEDICAL OFFICER IN THE ENGLISH CONVICT SERVICE
London, 1884

13
Sir Edmund Du Cane
THE PUNISHMENT AND PREVENTION OF CRIME
London, 1885

14
Louis Gordon Rylands
Crime: Its Causes and Remedy
London, 1888

15
William Tallack
Penological and Preventive Principles
London, 1889

16
Thomas Barwick Lloyd Baker
'War With Crime', Being a Selection of Reprinted Papers on Crime, Reformatories, etc.
London, 1889

17
Charles Tempest Clarkson and J. Hall Richardson.
Police!
London, 1889

18
Francis Scougal (Felicia Mary Frances Skene)
Scenes from a Silent World, or Prisons and Their Inmates
London, 1889

19
Andrew Lansdowne
A Life's Reminiscences of Scotland Yard
London, 1890

20
Arthur Griffiths
Secrets of the Prison-House, or
Gaol Studies and Sketches
London, 1894. Two volumes

21
William Douglas Morrison
Juvenile Offenders
London, 1896

22
Sir Robert Anderson
Criminals and Crime:
Some Facts and Suggestions
London, 1907

23
Thomas Holmes
Known to the Police
London, 1908

24
Richard F. Quinton
Crime and Criminals 1876–1910
London, 1910

25
Charles E. B. Russell
Young Gaol-Birds
London, 1910

26

James Devon

The Criminal and the Community

London, 1912

27

Sir Evelyn Ruggles-Brise

The English Prison System

London, 1921

28

Stephen Hobhouse and A. Fenner Brockway (eds.).

English Prisons To-day: Being the Report of the Prison System Enquiry Committee

London, 1922